Life Begins...

GW00703109

The comprehensive guide to enjoying living longer

Life Begins...

PROFESSOR STANLEY FELDMAN

metro

Published by Metro Publishing
An imprint of John Blake Publishing Ltd,
3 Bramber Court, 2 Bramber Road,
London W14 9PB, England

www.blake.co.uk

First published in paperback in 2007

ISBN 978-1-84454-399-1

British Library Cataloguing-in-Publication Data:

A catalogue record for this book is available from the British Library.

Design by www.envydesign.co.uk

Printed in the UK by CPI Bookmarque, Croydon, CR0 4TD

1 3 5 7 9 10 8 6 4 2

Cartoons by Mike Mosedale

Papers used by John Blake Publishing are natural, recyclable products made from
wood grown in sustainable forests. The manufacturing processes conform to the
environmental regulations of the country of origin.

To my family and friends who keep
me young at heart

Contents

Acknowledgements

This book is the culmination of many years' experience gained lecturing at the seminars and meetings run by The Retirement Trust. I would like to pay tribute to my fellow trustees and lecturers who work selflessly to explain to those approaching retirement how they can enjoy a full and healthy life.

I am particularly indebted to Stuart Robertson, of John Blake Publishing Ltd, whose helpful suggestions and advice has helped to shape this book and whose editing team have prevented me from indulging in any confusing technical jargon. I would like to thank Mike Mosedale for his cartoons which I hope will help the reader to contemplate the approach of the third age with a smile.

'Call themselves mature students !'

Preface

There is a revolution taking place that has barely been noticed: a seismic shift in the patterns of behaviour of those people now approaching retirement. Fifty years ago retirement was a short period of relief at the end of a working life, a time of 'being put out to grass' at the end of one's productive years. A person retiring at sixty to sixty-five years of age could expect this respite to last for little more than five to seven years. Even then, these last few years were often a time of limited mobility and ill health. In many, physical activity was restricted by a combination of chronic bronchitis, emphysema, rheumatism and arthritis. Others had the enjoyment of these years curtailed by a stroke or by heart failure. At sixty-five you were an old man or elderly lady and by and large you looked the part.

Today, the same person, retiring at the same age, will look and feel years younger and can reasonably anticipate twenty years of healthy life. The improvement in air quality, the reduction in smoking, the advent of joint-replacement surgery, antibiotics, anti-inflammatory drugs, hormone-replacement therapy and drugs to control blood pressure have greatly increased life expectancy and reduced the incidence of immobility and incapacity in the third age.

Today, for those prepared to embrace the opportunities that are around them, a new lease of life truly begins when their working life stops and they are no longer restricted by the routine of a work day existence. For them, life *begins* at retirement.

Introduction

Enjoy Living Longer

Those retiring today can expect to look forward to about twenty years of healthy, enjoyable life. Ageing has become merely a semantic concept and, for those who are prepared to challenge its effects, life after retirement has become a time of new experiences, new opportunities and new achievements. Although financial constraints and family commitments may prevent many from fully enjoying all the opportunities afforded by retirement, those retiring today are, in general, part of the lucky generation. They have the freedom to do what they like when they like. This has opened up the possibility for a change in their lifestyle that was not available to previous generations.

The coincidence of two quite separate developments has

put today's retirees in an especially fortunate position: better healthcare and the advent of globalisation.

Without the improvements that have taken place in public health and the benefits of advances in medicine and surgery, the present increase in life expectancy would not have occurred and the disability caused by ill health would have had a much greater effect on their ability to enjoy retirement.

Although the downside of globalisation is constantly stressed, it is because of the economies of scale, made possible by an international market, that today's retirees can enjoy pleasures and a level of comfortable living previously available only to the very rich. Many of these opportunities for new activities and new interests are presented in this book.

Nowhere is this change in today's lifestyle more apparent than in the annual wintertime exodus, by those no longer tethered to the routine of work, from the cold, damp, depressing days of winter to warmer, sunnier climes. Today, the urge to spend winter in the sun has spread throughout the whole of northern Europe and America. In ever-increasing numbers those freed from the anchor of the workplace migrate from the cold to the sunshine belt. They can be found in resorts in Florida in the West and throughout the Caribbean, the Canary Islands, the southern

Mediterranean, Africa, Asia and the Pacific. Today's retirees migrate in their hundreds and thousands as soon as the Christmas festivities are over, filling the aeroplanes, cars and coaches that leave our shores.

Their flight is like that of the wildebeest, whose annual migration takes them across the plains of Africa, or the birds that make their winter flight to warmer climes. They patiently tolerate the vicissitudes of the long journey for a few weeks in the sun. They take the queues at the borders, the jetlag and the foreign way of life in their stride as a price well worth paying to escape the rigours of a northern winter and a chance to enjoy the warmth of sunnier lands.

It is a lifestyle change that is set to grow. It provides many advantages that offset the cost of travel and accommodation. Winter is especially expensive in northern Europe, where the cost of heating and lighting is rising fast. It is a time when exercise tends to be restricted, and expensive and contagious diseases, especially upper-respiratory-tract infections and pneumonia, are more prevalent. The absence of clear sunny days followed by dark nights makes sleeping difficult due to its effect on melatonin, the sleep hormone. It is a good time to travel, since air fares tend to be lower in winter and there are many special deals available on off-season accommodation in the various holiday resorts.

Unfortunately, not all of these travellers are well prepared for the restrictions imposed by the effect of their increasing age upon the manner in which they can enjoy their winter in the sun. So it is that one finds retired travellers wondering about the risks to which they have suddenly become exposed. The new foods, the buffet lunches, the possibility of malaria and infectious diseases, the effect of heat and sunshine on their body, the increasing breathlessness when they climb up hills, the dizziness at high altitudes and the effects of age upon their joints and muscles. They need to know what precautions they should take and what activities should be curtailed.

There are many opportunities for a change in lifestyle once you have retired. However, if you are to enjoy your newfound freedom with safety and security it is necessary to recognise that increasing age causes alterations in your body that render you less vigorous and more vulnerable than when you were young.

Anyone contemplating retirement needs to be cautious, to recognise the limitations imposed by the ageing process and to heed advice. It is too easy, in the euphoria of retirement, to set oneself unreasonable objectives that overlook the inevitable changes taking place in one's body. No one would sensibly decide to take up weightlifting, mountaineering or competitive sprinting as a sport upon retirement. Although marathons have been run by ninety-year-old grandmothers, seventy-year-olds have climbed Everest and at least one ninety-year-old crossed the Atlantic in a small wooden boat, these feats were achieved by exceptional people and are beyond the capabilities of most of us.

This book is intended to make you aware of these changes so that you can anticipate them and minimise their impact upon your lifestyle. Most of these effects take place to our body, but changes also occur that affect our relationships with those around us. It is sensible to make provisions for those nearest and dearest and to understand the implications of wills and powers of attorney. Similarly, it is necessary to plan one's financial affairs prudently in order to avoid unnecessary anxiety in times of financial stress. To help address these widespread concerns, chapters on both these subjects, written by experts in the field, have been included.

So, this book does not attempt to provide a certain recipe for a happy retirement. There can be no universal panacea. Its objective is to point out the pitfalls that await the unwary, to warn of the difficulties involved in making the transition from work to retirement, and to provide advice on how to obtain the first prerequisite of a happy retirement: a healthy, sustainable lifestyle. It will help you to plan for a healthy and fulfilling retirement by establishing a lifestyle that uses your newfound freedom in a manner that you will find both rewarding and pleasurable so that you might enjoy living longer.

'Who are you calling an "old silver fox"?

Chapter One

Demographic Changes

We are living longer, healthier and more active lives. Only twenty-five years ago, the average life expectancy for a man was about sixty-nine years and there was a high probability that three out of every ten women would be immobile, or in some way physically handicapped, by the time they reached seventy-five. Today, the average life span for a women is over eighty years and most octogenarians enjoy an active lifestyle, thanks to healthier living and better medical care. It is estimated that within ten years about 25 per cent of the population of the UK will be over the age of sixty-five, with the biggest increase being in those between seventy-five and ninety-five years old. Surprisingly, although the absolute number of people living to be over a hundred has gone up, it has increased much less as a percentage of the population than would have been anticipated. It is almost as though nature had set a cut-off point for the length of one's life at around the hundred-year mark.

The economy is staggering under the effect of these demographic changes. In the past twenty years the number of men over fifty and in full-time employment has fallen from 86 per cent to 58 per cent. It has been estimated that about 40 per cent of those in full-time employment take early retirement and do not seek a further full-time job. This has resulted in about two and a half million people between fifty and sixty-five being economically inactive.

In the past, increased growth and personal savings mitigated the economic impact of these demographic changes. Today, when we have the prospect that within ten years it will require two people in work to support the needs of each retired pensioner, the government has started to realise the scale of the problem. Not only do pensioners rightly expect to enjoy the benefits of a lifestyle similar to that of someone in work, but they also cause a disproportionate burden on the state, as the provider of social and health care. In 2006 in the UK, there were about half a million people over the age of sixty-five in long-term full-time institutional care, and the same group constituted about 60 per cent of all hospital admissions. As a result most of the country's spending on healthcare goes on trying to fulfil the requirements of those in their last five years of life.

The changing patterns of employment and the increase in the number of those who are retired or not in full-time work have resulted in a vast army of people with time on their hands demanding leisure and recreational activities. Those who do not find any way of filling this time become bored, disillusioned and depressed as they struggle to leave behind the 'work ethic' they acquired over forty or so years of going to work. As a result, what should be a liberating experience – a chance to do *what* they wish *when* they wish – too often becomes a time of disappointment and frustration.

However, the consequence of the demographic effect of the increase in life expectancy has not been lost on the marketing industry. They have followed the growth of the over-sixties, whom they have dubbed 'the silver foxes', with interest.

Silver foxes are those people over sixty years old who have retired and who own their own house or flat. Many in this group find themselves with time on their hands and with money to indulge their whims. By and large, they have paid off their mortgages and, as a result of house price inflation, find that they possess an asset worth more than ten years' gross salary. Although they do not feel wealthy, because they no longer have a regular income, they have a sound and valuable cushion against financial adversity.

By the time you reach sixty and become a silver fox, your children are usually grown up and independent; they are no longer a financial liability. You do not have to put money aside for school fees, uniforms, holidays and other expenses. Silver foxes find making ends meet easier than they had anticipated. Now they are retired, they do not have to spend money to keep up appearances; they do not need to dress up to go to work; they can enjoy wearing casual clothes and they can save money by doing odd jobs about the house themselves.

One can see why the marketing men have decided that this group constitute a potentially lucrative pool of customers and a target for mail-order firms. They have identified certain general trends in this population. They tend to be overindulgent to grandchildren, often denying themselves luxuries in order to do so. The men love gadgets. They buy these toys on impulse, even though they often have no present use for them. However, they are bad at reading and following instructions unless they are straightforward. As a result, at the first sign of any difficulty, they abandon the device. The women tend to turn their interest from fashion magazines to lifestyle ones; they spend more time and money on the grandchildren; and they seek more interests outside the home.

While the marketing fraternity have been quick to cotton on to the economic importance of the over-sixties, the politicians have not been far behind. In any election, focus groups have been obliged to concern themselves with the perceived requirements of the 'grey vote'. Promises of better pension provision for the elderly (usually so far in the future that few of those at present retired will live to see the benefits) and assistance to meet the rising cost of heating and council taxes become a standard mantra of all the political parties. The vote of the over-sixties is essential for electoral success. We are beginning to see the rise of their political influence, although it has not reached the importance it enjoys in the USA.

The group that has been slowest to recognise the opportunities provided by what has been loosely referred to as the 'third age' are those who actually make up its numbers. There are organisations representing those sections of this population who have failed to prepare themselves, financially or legally, for the changes that occur once they stop regular employment. However, to most silver foxes, entering the third age is, as we have noted, seen as being 'put out to grass', as being at the end of one's useful existence, and, consequently, it is often a time of depression and despair. In a survey carried out between 2004 and 2006 on people attending pre-retirement seminars it was found that many more participants were concerned about how they would fill their days in order to avoid boredom than were worried about the loss of a regular income.

There is little doubt that the prospect of imminent retirement imposes a huge psychological stress on most people although they are reluctant to admit to it. Too little is done to help them to see the opportunities and challenges that retirement can bring and that it need not be a time of 'running down'. As a result of the failure to prepare for retirement, many people who have eagerly anticipated an end to the treadmill of their working life find that, when retirement actually comes, they are fearful in case they will not know what to do with themselves.

There can be little doubt that the anxieties and the aspirations of the over-sixties vary according to financial and social circumstances. Those with only the state pension, living in rented accommodation, are never going to have the same opportunities or priorities as someone with a good pension and a substantial nest egg. Nevertheless, irrespective of the circumstances, as one nears the age of sixty it is sensible to take precautions to prepare oneself for the inevitable changes that will occur upon retirement in order to enjoy a healthy lifestyle that avoids unnecessary mental stress and needless expense.

Today, the demographic changes that have occurred mean that the third age, for most of the over-sixties, will last for about twenty years. It is foolish not to plan for that period of one's life in order to ensure that it is healthy, productive and fulfilling. To enter this period hoping that 'something will turn up' is a recipe for disaster. Retirement needs planning that takes into account the altered needs of everyday living and the physical changes that take place in one's body as one gets older.

'In my day, so-called "great tenors" didn't mumble their arias.'

Chapter Two

The Consequences of Retirement

Depression

Most of us get depressed from time to time. Like the emotions of joy and sorrow, this type of depression is a normal response. It results from our inability to control the world around us. It is a reaction to changes, or circumstances, that upset our personal sense of wellbeing. Such depression is normal. It is an almost inevitable consequence of retirement.

Suddenly, upon retirement, one becomes a nonperson. The loss of one's sense of being required and of one's status as the wage earner becomes apparent. It might be triggered off by a telephone call at work, asking for the pass to the company car park to be handed in, or by seeing a successor's name on the door of the office. With it comes the realisation that one is entering the third age, growing old and losing power and influence. Inevitably one's thoughts turn to the depressing fact that there is no fourth age.

There is no doubt that these thoughts figure more prominently in the minds of men than women. Men usually have a more developed ego drive than women and they find it more difficult to come to terms with the loss of status following retirement than women, who rank security as being more important than power. Nevertheless, depression is commonplace once the farewell party is over and the long-service clock has been placed on the mantelpiece. Because it is commonplace, it's important to recognise its symptoms. Understanding the problem puts you in charge of its treatment, while failure to recognise the symptoms for what they are leads to unnecessary visits to the doctor, domestic friction and the development of abnormal, pathological, depressive states, which require professional intervention.

Confidence

Loss of confidence is a common symptom of depression; it manifests itself in different ways in different individuals. It may present itself as a reluctance to initiate something new, such as to telephone a friend, meet new people or invite friends to a dinner party, for fear of a rebuttal. Gradually, victims retreat further and further into themselves, seeming to prefer their own company, until the very thought of going out to meet friends or going to the cinema becomes an insurmountable emotional hurdle. This symptom becomes self-perpetuating, because the best cure lies in developing friendships and exploring new opportunities.

If sufferers realise that this reluctance to participate in normal social events is a symptom of depression, they can be helped and encouraged to overcome this reticence. Self-confidence can usually be regained by adopting a regular routine of getting up at a set time every day, entertaining friends on a regular basis, taking part in joint projects such as art classes, evening classes or the University of the Third Age (often called the U3A), or becoming involved in new sporting activities. Failure to come to terms with the loss of confidence will result in the patient becoming an emotional hermit.

Perchance to dream!

Sleeplessness, especially the tendency to wake up in the early hours of the morning with one's mind in turmoil, is a common depressive symptom. This is especially true when it coincides with a loss of confidence. Sufferers often spend hour after hour in the middle of the night debating with themselves why the world is not to their liking. In the short term the condition can be met by taking a sleeping pill to get over a particular precipitating event. The danger is that the sleeping pills may become a prop that maintains the depressive state and come to be seen as essential in order to face the night. Alternative measures, such as warm milky drinks and reading, may help but the most effective treatment is for someone to listen sympathetically to the depressed person's perceived troubles until he or she comes to see them in perspective. Unfortunately, this often means that *two* people end up having a poor night's sleep.

I don't believe it! The Victor Meldrew syndrome

The grumpy old man portrayed by Richard Wilson as Victor Meldrew in the popular BBC television sitcom *One Foot in the Grave* is typical of the depressive syndrome. Rather than admit to himself that his problems are due to his own inability to come to terms with his new lifestyle, he blames those around him for his feelings of being unwanted and rejected. Any feeling of frustration and every disappointment is projected on to his wife or his 'ungrateful children'. Unfortunately, it usually produces a retaliatory response, which then appears to justify the initial accusations.

The sad effect of this depressive symptom is the loss of the sympathy of the very person who is in a position to offer help. It's the cause of the breakdown of many marriages soon after retirement. It is important to realise that the accusations of these grumpy old men are intended to wound and to produce a response that will confirm that the reason they feel miserable is someone else's fault. They don't necessarily reflect any genuine ill feeling or hostility. Once the depression passes, these outbursts tend to stop.

Alcoholism

While there are many reasons why those entering the third age tend to increase their alcohol intake, it is the depressive who usually risks becoming a true alcoholic. Alcohol has always been a means of escaping from reality when the world is not to one's liking, but in the depressive it may too easily become a way of life. It is important to recognise it for what it is: a symptom of a failure to make the adaptations necessary for the change from work to retirement. If regular alcohol consumption starts to increase to more than four units a day it should be restricted to the evenings, preferably after dinner. A more active and interesting lifestyle is the first requisite if the condition is to be reversed.

Loss of appetite and libido

Although depressives frequently complain they are never hungry and tend to peck at any meal that is put before them, they usually maintain or increase their weight. This is particularly common in women who face their meals with little enthusiasm but who graze on the contents of the fridge all day long. It's symptomatic of the lack of enthusiasm that typifies the depressive. A similar disinclination to indulge in anything that normal people regard as pleasurable applies to sex. The depressive has a greatly reduced libido.

Aches, pains and headaches

There is little doubt that many of the older patients who flock to doctors' surgeries complaining of vague aches and pains, of headaches and muscle weakness, are suffering from a depression. The problem for the doctor is that in some patients these symptoms may be due to an organic illness. The difficulty is in deciding which are which. Making the diagnosis with any degree of certainty requires taking a detailed history, examining the patient and, often, performing expensive tests. This is very time-consuming and, as a result, a patient who's just retired is too often labelled as suffering from depression and given antidepressants without first excluding the possibility of organic pathology.

The most important part of the treatment of depression is to get the patient to accept the true cause of the problems. Only then will he or she become amenable to taking the steps necessary to overcome the depression. Patients must be encouraged to see the positive opportunities that present themselves, if only they can be stirred into action.

Post-retirement depression requires sympathy, under-standing and patience. It is most readily treated within the supportive environment of a happy marriage or other stable partnership surrounded by longstanding friends. Because depressives feel unwell, there's a tendency to try to escape from the situation by going on holiday in the belief that once they're away from home they'll feel better and their problems will go away. This is a mistake. Too often it proves to be a time for brooding rather than facing up to the necessary changes in lifestyle that are required. Not only does it not cure the depression but also it usually results in a miserable, quarrelsome holiday that increases family tensions and recriminations.

If the depression starts to interfere with normal life, if there's a reluctance to get up in the morning and to participate in normal social intercourse and if there is a threat of self-harm, you should seek professional help.

Boredom

Boredom came out top of the list of 'fears' that were recorded by those attending the pre-retirement seminars mentioned in Chapter 1. After forty or so years of working life, the work ethic becomes so ingrained that even going to the pictures in the afternoon feels like an illicit, subversive activity. If you can, it's sensible to wean yourself off this addiction to work in the years before the working routine finally comes to an end. It may be possible to achieve this by the three-day weekend, the shorter working day or more frequent holidays, especially if you're self-employed.

But for most people there's little or no provision for a gradual transition from work to retirement. Where it *is* possible, it should be seized upon as a chance to encompass new activities, join affinity-group pursuits such as bridge clubs, book clubs, the University of the Third Age or collectors' circles, and to edge your way slowly into an alternative lifestyle once the time for retirement arrives. Other pursuits might be one or more of the following:

- amateur theatre or operatic groups
- night classes, whether car mechanics, creative, writing or computers (get to grips with the Internet)
- online activities such as forums, special-interest groups
- aerobics and keep-fit classes

- golf and other sports clubs
- pub activities such as quizzes and darts teams
- caravan clubs
- gardening and allotment organisations
- handicrafts

One of the unfortunate effects of modern society is that many wives and female partners have careers, too. Because they have often been interrupted by child rearing, they tend to peak later than those of their spouses. This, together with the probability that the wife is younger than her husband, means that, when the man reaches retirement, the female half of the relationship is reaching her maximum working potential. Understandably, she's starting to enjoy work and doesn't want to retire, so, sadly, the man's left at home alone during the week without the company he's been used to every weekend throughout his working life. A sure recipe for boredom.

There is no universal prescription to prevent time hanging heavily on the hands of the recently retired. They have exchanged a rigidly structured working life for one that has no signposts or boundaries. It's sensible to ensure that the new lifestyle also sets limits and parameters. This can be achieved in different ways to suit the circumstances of each individual.

Try dividing the year into blocks, punctuated by breaks away from the home environment. These can consist of two or three holidays a year. At least one of these should be in winter, when long, dark days spent at home are both depressing and expensive. Whenever possible they should be active and educational.

It's a good idea to punctuate the rest of the year with long weekends of two or three days away from home, either with friends or family. The week should also be divided up with as many set fixtures as possible, whether these be in voluntary work, group activities such as bridge, golf or evening classes, or simply a morning a week to pay the bills and do the household accounts. Many find it helps to establish the new lifestyle if they divide up the day so that the mornings are devoted to household chores, the afternoons to exercise and the evenings to entertainment. The actual pursuits don't matter; what *is* important in overcoming boredom and the feeling that there's nothing to look forward to, is having a set routine for each week.

People find satisfaction from very different pursuits. There are a great number of voluntary organisations that are crying out for help. Those with a particular professional skill may find that organisations such as Reach will put them in touch with charities that need extra help (see Appendix C, 'Useful Addresses'). Many who have brought up their own children enjoy voluntary teaching in schools or helping to supervise children's holidays. Most public libraries carry details of these opportunities. Further-education classes and the U3A provide an excellent opportunity to meet people and to acquire new skills and knowledge. (A word of caution: remember that your memory could deteriorate with age, so, if you're at all worried on that score, you may wish to think twice about enrolling on a course that puts a premium on remembering facts and figures.)

It is a mistake to become too closely involved in looking after grandchildren. It's tempting to drop everything in response to a call from children whose babysitter has let them down. Suddenly, you're needed. While there's no need to deny yourself the pleasure of helping out with the grandchildren from time to time, take care that it doesn't become a way of life. Too often it ends up with the grandparents spending so much time and energy looking after their grandchildren that they neglect their friends and ignore their acquaintances. All they can then talk about when they meet their friends is their grandchildren; they become boring. Once the grandchildren reach their teens the grandparents often find themselves bereft of friends when, as inevitably occurs, their grand-children want the company of their peers. This can be disastrous. It is your friends and acquaintances who play an essential role in widening your interests and who provide intellectual stimulation as you get older.

Loss of friends

It is inevitable that your circle of friends will be drawn mainly from those you work with. This bond of work is lost on retirement. Workplace gossip and news no longer have the same importance or interest once you've retired. While many friendships survive this rupture, some acquaintance-ships will be lost. The fear of no longer being one of the boys or girls, of being regarded as yesterday's person, is commonplace on retirement, especially among the 'blokier' men. The reminiscences of the retiree soon pall when he or she turns up in the pub to meet old friends after work and starts talking about 'the old days' or 'in my time'. As retirement approaches, you should ensure that your friends are drawn from as many different environments as possible so you have convivial company without having to haunt the place where you used to work.

It's easy to see the negative side of retirement, but this often obscures the potential positive benefits it offers, with the opportunity to widen your interests, to do new things, to make new friend and to take holidays at times when travel is cheap and hotels less crowded. It is important to accept that changes in your lifestyle are inevitable and necessary, but if they're anticipated and exploited, you can look forward to a positive, enjoyable third age.

Just as important as coming to terms with the changes that will inevitably occur on retirement is the recognition of the changes that happen as your body gets older. Appreciating the nature of these changes allows you to adopt a lifestyle that will help you to keep fit and healthy so that you can enjoy the benefits of retirement.

'George's retirement last year hasn't quite sunk in.'

Chapter Three

When and Where to Retire

There's pressure on the government to legislate for both men and women to continue working until they are between 65 and 70. This is understandable, since life expectancy is increasing every year, while the size of the labour force is failing to increase fast enough to keep pace with the increased demand. Without some such adjustment there wouldn't be enough people in work and paying taxes to support those who have retired. This is made worse by the falling population of most European countries as a result of the diminishing birth rate. In some countries the age at which a person decides to retire is left to the worker, but in all European countries there is a minimum age at which a person can retire on a full pension.

While there are obvious economic advantages to the country of working until one drops, there are disadvantages that should be considered before a fixed age for retirement is established. The most important disadvantage of postponing retirement is that, in certain circumstance, it can be dangerous to employees or to the company or organisation for which they work. It is essential that the social and health implications of working longer should be considered before a fixed retirement age is set. Even then, the effects of a premature deterioration in a particular faculty that may be essential for the safe performance of a person's work might necessitate flexibility.

Some types of work are more demanding of skills that are prone to the effect of ageing than others. In these circumstances prolonging the working life may put people's lives at risk and place an undue stress upon the employee. It's better not to set a fixed, catch-all retirement age but rather, for economic reasons, to set a *minimum pensionable* retirement age.

There may be good reasons why airline pilots are encouraged to retire from flying at fifty-five, but the present arrangements, whereby psychiatrists retire at this age, are absurd. As the age of sixty approaches, one's ability to think rapidly and to recall instructions becomes slowed. This phenomenon is seen in quiz shows such as

Mastermind, where the older contestants struggle to recall information quickly from the recesses of their brains. The rate at which this slowing down occurs varies enormously from person to person. To prevent any possible harmful consequence in all employees would require a very young, catch-all retirement age. Clearly, such a course is impracticable and undesirable.

The more sensible approach to this problem would be to transfer anyone in a job that required a particular skill – a skill that would be affected by their growing older – to one that placed an emphasis on experience and accumulated wisdom. This problem is commonly seen in certain medical specialties, where a deadline of sixty-five for retirement is generally accepted. The records of the various medical organisations dealing with complaints against doctors show that these complaints increase dramatically when the doctor reaches the age of sixty. This is a reflection of the difficulty of keeping abreast of new techniques and embracing change as one gets older.

The tendency is for one's interests to become increasingly narrow so that one knows more and more about less and less. There is also an inevitable loss of manual dexterity and visual acuity, so that procedures such as arterial surgery, requiring fine movements and good eyesight, become increasingly difficult. Nevertheless, if all doctors retired at sixty it would cause a tragic loss of the many years of experience in a profession that is short of trained staff. It would be preferable to offer these doctors the opportunity to transfer to administrative or organisational duties.

Trying to keep up with younger, more nimble colleagues, with better eyesight and steadier hands, can impose an enormous stress on those who feel that their own performance is deteriorating. This realisation may cause mental or physical illness and a dramatic reduction in life expectancy. It has been found that doctors who continue to work until the retirement age of sixty-five years have a shorter life expectancy than those who retire at sixty. On the other hand, managers, working in the same environment, whose performance and confidence generally increase as they get older, live longer if they retire later.

This inconsistent pattern is found in many occupations and makes it impossible to set an appropriate fixed age for retirement for all workers. Any sign of a loss of confidence or a deterioration in the worker's health record should alert an employer to the realisation that the time has come either to change the nature of the employees job or to advise early retirement.

In the USA, the age-discrimination laws make it impossible to terminate the contracts of workers against their will on the basis of age. Similar laws are being considered by the EU. While this has many benefits for workers, who can virtually set their own date for retirement, it can prove to be a burden on a company or a research institution. For an employee, it is often possible to take advantage of this law to ease themselves slowly into retirement, by working part-time. The problem comes when an elderly academic or a senior partner refuses to relinquish their position and blocks the advancement of a successor.

Ideally, each person approaching retirement should be able to enjoy a period of diminished responsibility, or a shorter working week, to give them the opportunity to prepare for their new life. Unfortunately, this is seldom possible, since in most institutions there's a need to plan for the replacement of ageing staff well in advance of their retirement.

It is becoming increasingly obvious that, although it may be socially desirable for women to retire at an earlier age than men, economic and actuarial considerations make this impossible without imposing a pension penalty. Indeed, taking into account any time spent out of employment raising children and the longer life that can be anticipated by a female, a case can be made for women to retire at a later age than men! The equitable alternative would be for them to work for fewer years than men but to make higher contributions each year to their pension insurance.

The decision about the best age to retire depends upon many factors: employees' health, for instance, their financial circumstances, any pension advantages, their ability to cope with the stress of the job, their desire to do something different while they're still young enough. Unfortunately, for most people the decision is taken out of their hands and dictated by a contract of employment or an agreement between their employer and their union.

Where to live

Some people facing retirement feel a need for a complete break with their working life and a new start in a different environment, often in a new country. They seek to escape from familiar surroundings and to start their new life in a sunnier, warmer place. Each year thousands flee the British climate, with its long, dark winter days, for the Mediterranean coast of Spain or France. A recent survey found that more than 40 per cent of them find the change so traumatic that they return home to familiar surroundings and to their friends within five years. It proves to be an expensive mistake.

A similar picture is found when someone who has lived in a large town all their life decides to seek the 'good life' and settle down in a small rural hamlet where they can cultivate their own plot of land and keep livestock. The experiment is doomed to failure. Only those who take the trouble to put down roots by repeatedly visiting the site of their dream home before they retire are likely to succeed. Unless they have established some contacts and have some idea of the likely structure of the new life awaiting them in their new home, the lack of close friends with a common interest causes a sense of loneliness and isolation, leading to misery and regret.

Anyone contemplating retiring to a place in the sun should be able to hold a conversation in the native language of the country and to have established friendships with some of the people living in the area. Relocating to a rural idyll can be equally difficult unless you've taken the trouble to put down roots before retiring. It's too easy to forget that, in the long dark winter days, you need entertaining and stimulating companionship. Days of continuous rain can be daunting, sealed up in a country cottage without any friends. Inevitably, the newcomer to a community is an outsider and any new acquaintance may prove to be a poor substitute for the old friends with whom they have many shared experiences.

'He just can't stand being called a pensioner!'

Chapter Four

The Inside Story: Internal Ageing Processes

Most of the cells that make up the organs of our bodies have reached their maximum development potential by the time we are in our early teens and they have started the slow process of degeneration by the time we reach maturity. For most of our adult life we more than compensate for the reduced efficiency of the cells responsible for our bodily functions by patterns of behaviour that we acquire by experience. Nevertheless, the underlying changes of ageing continue remorselessly, eating into the margin of safety provided by the large reserve capacity that exists in most of the organs of the body. These effects are, for the most part, irreversible.

The rate at which these changes occur varies from person

to person so that, although the general trends can be predicted, the extent of the change found at any time varies from one individual to another. There is a strong genetic influence over this process, but the general health of the individual and the strains imposed by the environment also affect the rate at which the ageing process takes place. Because you're your parents' child, you can often guess at the rate and the degree of the ageing you're likely to experience due to genetics by observing its effect on Mum and Dad.

Some technical stuff: changes at a cellular level

I'll try not to get *too* bogged down in detail here, but some explanation is needed. At birth, the chromosomes in the nucleus of the body's cells have a large amount of unscripted capacity that appears to be surplus to requirements. Much of this is in the tail of the chromosome and constitutes what's known as the *telomere*. A telomere is a region of DNA that has a protective function during replication. During life, the length of these telomeres decreases and their shape and size come to vary. It's believed that the rate of these changes is greatly accelerated by exposure to *free radicals* (highly reactive atoms or groups of atoms) produced by various chemical processes within the cells.

This is the basis of the assumption – one that, in spite of

many extravagant claims based on many epidemiological studies, is scientifically unproven – that eating foods rich in *antioxidants* can prevent the ravages of age and the many age-related diseases. Antioxidants are substances that prevent oxidation, and oxidation can be destructive. In a test tube, antioxidants can be shown to mop up and neutralise the free radicals.

It's possible that the disruption of the tail of the chromosome leads to the uncontrolled activity in the nuclei of the cells, causing cancer to develop. It would explain why the prevalence of cancer increases with age and the role free radicals, such as those caused by prolonged exposure to ionising radiation, play in its causation.

There are exceptions to this ageing process: the chromosomes in the nucleus of the ova (reproductive cells) and the sperm are spared it. These special cells contain a protective enzyme called *telomerase*, which repairs any destruction of the telomere. As a result, ova and sperm cells do not age as readily as the rest of the cells of the body. Dramatic proof of this came with the cloning of a ewe and the birth of Dolly the sheep. She was cloned from cells taken from the skin of her mother's breast. Since the mother was a mature animal, the ageing process was already well advanced in the cell from which Dolly was cloned. In effect, Dolly was born with the cells containing the telomeres of a grown-up animal. The result was that Dolly aged rapidly, and she died prematurely. Had she been born after a pseudo-fertilisation of an ovum she would probably have lived a normal life span.

Other effects of ageing within the cell cause a reduction in enzymatic activity. Because of this the metabolism of food and drugs is generally slower in older people and the effects of substances, such as alcohol, last longer.

Working against this effect is the process known as *enzyme induction*, in which the enzyme activity is ratcheted up by repeated exposure to a particular type of drug. In spite of enzyme induction, which works on one special enzyme system in the liver, the effects of many drugs tend to be prolonged in the elderly so that if they are given on a regular daily basis they run the risk of accumulating in the body. This is particularly true of long-acting drugs such as Valium, which can accumulate and cause confusion and drowsiness if given to older patients on a daily basis.

Cell division and reproduction tends to slow down as you get older. This effect varies enormously from tissue to tissue, but in general it results in reduced healing powers. Wounds take longer to heal and they tend to do so with fibrous scar tissue rather than with cells that are active. This effect is commonly seen after plastic surgery, where the usual, almost invisible scars tend to be thicker and occasionally puckered. This reduced ability to produce new cells, especially if they serve a specialised function, makes it difficult to develop replacements for those lost. It makes it difficult to build up muscle cells in order to increase your muscle bulk as you get older, however much you exercise. The most you can achieve by exercise is to maintain the tone and power of existing muscles. No amount of weightlifting will produce the bulging biceps and powerful pecs found in a younger person once you've reached the third age.

The body's response to blood loss and infections is reduced and slowed with ageing. It takes longer to replace red blood corpuscles lost after a haemorrhage, and the immune response of the lymphocytes, an essential part of fighting infections, is decreased. Any cells damaged by an infective process are likely to be replaced by scar tissue. As a result, if an infection results in the loss of cells that serve a particular protective purpose – such as may occur with the loss of the specialised cells lining the breathing passages during pneumonia – it may cause permanent impairment of function and a reduction in the body's protective mechanisms.

Body content

As we get older, the amount of water in the body decreases as a proportion of body weight. We literally dry out. As a result of the loss of fluid, the skin becomes less elastic. If you gently pinch the skin of an elderly person it stays in a heap, returning only slowly to its normal shape. Compare this with the skin of young person, where the elasticity prevents it from becoming 'pinched up'.

The loss of water is one of the factors contributing to the development of facial wrinkles, but it also affects other bodily structures. Possibly the most dramatic effect comes from the loss of water in the fluid cushions that separate the vertebrae. As these intervertebral discs contribute about 20 per cent of the length of the vertebral column, the effect of their shrinkage is to reduce the patient's height. This is one of the principal causes of the inevitable loss of stature in the elderly.

The amount of fat as a proportion of body weight increases. Some tissues develop a fatty infiltration. This is seen particularly in muscle that is not regularly exercised. Elastic tissue is also lost and replaced by inelastic fibrous tissue. The replacement of elastic by inelastic fibrous tissue is the main cause of facial ageing, as it causes the wrinkles that characterise age. The loss of the elasticity in the tissues around the eye and in the nasolabial furrow, the groove between the nose and the corner of the mouth, causes the characteristic facial appearance of middle age. It is these changes that surgical facelift operations aim to correct.

The loss of elastic tissue occurs in all the organs of the body. The loss of elasticity in the main arteries of the body inevitably causes the blood pressure to rise in the elderly. The aorta of young people is like a bicycle inner tube. Its walls contain a thick layer of elastic tissue. Because of this elasticity it distends when blood is ejected into it at each beat of the heart, cushioning the force produced by the contraction of the heart muscle and reducing the rise in pressure that would otherwise occur.

As you get older, the loss of elasticity in your blood vessels causes them to act more like a rigid pipe than an elastic tube. As a result there is a steep rise in blood pressure each time the heart contracts. A similar loss of elastic tissue occurs in the heart itself and this, together with the replacement of muscle with scar tissue and fat, causes a reduction in its ability to adapt to an increase in demand by dilating and ejecting more blood with each beat.

The general replacement of elastic and muscle tissue with inelastic fibrous tissue is also responsible for the deterioration of eyesight that occurs with age.

Fatty infiltration and loss of muscle tone are responsible for the reduced control of sphincters, such as those required for the retention of gas in the rectum. It causes the weakening of the muscular sphincters of the pelvic floor that are responsible for preventing urinary incontinence, especially in women, as they get older.

There is a tendency to lose calcium from bones as one gets older. This effect occurs most readily in the long bones such as those of the arms and legs. It also occurs in the vertebrae. At the same time, other bones, called the *membrane bones* – so called because they develop in membranes whose evolutionary history can be traced back to the scales of fish and the shells of turtles – tend to become denser and heavier with age.

The decalcification of the 'cartilaginous' long bones is one of the few effects of ageing that are to some extent reversible. It can be minimised by exercises that put pressure on the bones or stress them. In women it is influenced by the reduction in oestrogen in the blood that occurs at the menopause. This can be offset by hormone-replacement therapy (HRT). The calcification process is controlled by a hormone secreted by four tiny parathyroid glands situated in the neck, immersed in the thyroid. The effectiveness of its activity can be enhanced by drug therapy to prevent or limit the loss of bone density.

The deposition of cholesterol in the walls of arteries starts at a fairly early age but its effects become noticeable only in later life. In men, ageing is associated with an enlargement of the prostate gland at the neck of the bladder, which may produce difficulty in urination. The whorls of tissue that develop in benign prostatic enlargement are infiltrated with dense deposits of cholesterol. It is possible that this effect may, in time, be reduced now that statins – drugs that block the local production of cholesterol – are widely used.

The brain is also affected by the ageing process (more on this in Chapter 6). Its cells, like those of all other metabolically active tissue, slow down with age. It produces less of the transmitter chemicals that are essential for its cells to communicate with one another and to pass their messages on to the organs of the body. In a gross form it causes Parkinson's disease, senile dementia, Alzheimer's disease and the dizziness and faintness that is occasionally experienced on getting out of bed or standing up after a heavy meal. In the less severe but more insidious form it causes memory loss and a shakiness of the extended hand.

Alzheimer's disease and age-related memory loss

Alzheimer's disease is a condition called presenile dementia. This is a rapidly progressive dementia that occurs in people who are young to middle-aged. Its causation and its pathology are very different from the loss of memory and general forgetfulness that occurs as one gets older. True Alzheimer's disease causes premature death, whereas the memory loss of older people is compatible with a normal life expectancy.

It is generally accepted that the changes that occur as we get older are due to a running down of the chemical transmitters by means of which the cells of the brain talk to one another. The more complex cerebral circuits, such as those involved in recall, are principally affected. The newer memory that has not been bedded down by repeated use is affected more readily than the memory for distant events. It particularly affects the loss of recall for names.

Although certain mental exercises have been devised to help in remembering events and names, none are universally beneficial. The more one uses any function in the brain, the better it is likely to function. Word games and puzzles, crosswords and Scrabble may assist in developing one's memory. Some people find that drugs that prevent the destruction of neurotransmitters are helpful in preventing short-term memory failure.

The condition is made worse by alcohol and sleeping pills. It was found during tests carried out on climbers ascending Mount Everest that those people who overbreathe in order to adapt to high altitudes, or other conditions of low oxygen saturation, are more likely to suffer memory loss. This may also happen after anaesthetics in which the patient is paralysed and artificially hyper-ventilated and after cardiopulmonary bypass or cardiac surgery. It is known that, when high concentrations of oxygen are administered for any length of time, the blood vessels to the brain may contract. This would be expected to make any memory loss worse.

Undoubtedly, the most important way of minimising the effects of the age-related memory loss is by regular involvement in intelligent conversation and argument. Loneliness and isolation, either individually or as a couple, aggravates the condition. This underlines the importance of maintaining one's network of friends as one gets older.

The body's immune system becomes less and less effective with age. As a result, its ability to fight infections is reduced. As a consequence, not only does it become more difficult to overcome infections, but also organisms that are unlikely to cause serious disease in the young fit person can cause life-threatening problems in older people. Influenza tends to turn into pneumonia in the elderly and upper respiratory infections are more likely to infect the chest. Legionnaires' disease, which is seldom fatal in the young, carries a high mortality in the elderly.

Blood clots occur more readily in the elderly, causing an increased risk of deep-vein thrombosis and stroke (we'll look in more detail at deep-vein thrombosis in Chapter 16, 'Holidays and Travel'). This is to some extent the effect of the physiological dehydration that occurs, but there is also an element of increased platelet stickiness involved.

(Platelets are tiny blood particles that play an important part in clotting.)

It is these slow but inevitable changes that occur with ageing that prevent us from being as adaptable or strong as we were when we were young. However, the slow pace of many of these changes allows us to make subtle changes in lifestyle so as to minimise any inconvenience they may cause. It is important to appreciate the changes for what they are, the effect of ageing, and to accept them as normal and not as signs of a disease or impending senility.

Living with the changes

The difficulty of reversing the changes associated with ageing does not mean that they should necessarily interfere with the enjoyment of life. It is the changes that inevitably occur within the nuclei of the cells of the body that cause us to age and predispose our bodies to an increased risk of developing cancer. They cannot readily be inhibited or reversed. There are frequent claims that this or that food prevents ageing and cancer. These reports are usually based on the limited epidemiological observations that people eating a particular food live longer than those who have a different diet. There is little scientific evidence to support most of these claims. However, there is good evidence that certain ethnic groups tend to live longer than others. This effect is more likely to be linked to their genetic makeup than to the way they live or the food they eat.

Although there are some cancers that occur almost exclusively in children and young people, in most cases cancer is a disease of old age. Because the population is living longer and, thanks to better hygiene and antibiotics, no longer dying in large numbers from infective diseases, it is almost certain that the proportion of the population dying of cancer will increase in the future.

Antioxidant drugs and foods have been advocated as a means of providing some degree of protection against chromosomal destruction. Red wine, vitamin C and various food additives have been claimed to reduce cancer risks in the elderly. Whether they do work is doubtful. It is difficult to see how the antioxidant chemicals they contain can manage to get into the nuclei of the cells in sufficient quantities to affect the ageing process materially. However, they do appear to be harmless, even if the claims for their usefulness are exaggerated.

The realisation that the third age is associated with physical deterioration and is the time of life when one becomes increasingly vulnerable to disease leads many to seek to try to protect themselves from the inevitable by potions, pills, special cult totems, absurd diets and extreme ways of life. Each year the over-fifties spend billions of pounds on herbal remedies, special diets, vitamin pills, yoga and meditation, and such unlikely remedies as rectal enemas, sleeping with a magnet under the bed or wearing coloured beads. In spite of anecdotal evidence and clever marketing there is little evidence that any of these 'cult pursuits' are of any benefit to anyone other than those purveying these snake-oil treatments.

At present there is no single food, medicine or drug that has been shown in any scientific study to prolong life or slow cellular ageing – if there were, we would all be taking them! However, by following a sensible lifestyle based on an appreciation of the changes that are happening as we get older, the effects of these cellular events can be minimised and in some cases reversed. Before we can do this it is necessary to see just how the changes that accompany ageing affect the way our body works.

'I've been using your product for over 20 years now...
when is it going to start working?'

Chapter Five

On the Outside: Visible Changes

Look at a picture of yourself as a teenager or young adult, and you see immediately how the passage of time has produced noticeable changes in your appearance. It's because of these changes that we can guess at a person's age. If they occurred consistently, at the same rate in everyone, we would be able to make this guess with some accuracy, but because the rate of ageing varies, influenced by genetic and environmental factors, our guessing ability is of limited accuracy.

The shape of the body, the appearance of wrinkles and furrows on the face, changes in the texture of the skin, the loss of hair, the diminution in height and the way we move are all giveaway signs of the ageing process

Shape of the body

The process by which we lose height starts insidiously at forty to sixty years of age. It gathers pace as we get older, becoming most noticeable in those over seventy. It is largely due to the loss of water in the body and especially in the intervertebral discs. The larger or more numerous the intervertebral discs in a particular part of the body, the greater this squashing effect has on height.

This process is exaggerated in later life by some degree of imploding of the vertebrae. It is common to find collapsed or wedged vertebrae in people over seventy. This is particularly true in postmenopausal women, where the decalcification that occurs in the vertebrae in the thoracic (chest) region causes them to become wedge-shaped and to produce the so-called 'dowager's hump'. Today, with HRT and other means of treating osteoporosis in women, this condition is less commonly seen. In men, the process tends to occur more slowly and over a more protracted period. Although there have been advocates of HRT for men, the fear of the risk of causing an increase in the incidence of cancer of the prostate has prevented it from being generally accepted.

The effect of the loss of height is that a body of the same size has to be squeezed into a shorter frame. It invariably results in an increase in diameter or girth. This effect is most noticeable in the lumbar region, where it causes some degree of potbelly, often incorrectly referred to as a 'beer belly'. It is also noticeable in the neck, which becomes shortened, causing an increase in collar size. Any wedging of the vertebrae exaggerates the tendency of older people to become 'round-shouldered'. This effect is often made worse by the rigidity that occurs as adjacent vertebrae fuse, which, in itself, makes the process of straightening one's back difficult and painful.

Not all bones lose calcium or become smaller. The bones of the head, especially those that make up the cranium, or skull, become denser and slightly larger, causing an increase in hat-band size. This effect is not seen in the bones of the jaw, which become more fragile and decalcified in older people. This often precipitates the loss of teeth, which tends to exacerbate the sunken-in look of the mouth that is associated with ageing.

We can now understand the process underlying the typical appearance of the elderly. It is important to recognise these changes for what they are and to minimise their impact on your enjoyment of life. Is there anything we can do about it? Stretching and bending exercises carried out frequently and enthusiastically can delay the manifestations of these effects, but they will not prevent them. HRT in women certainly helps to put off these effects, although it will not ultimately prevent them in the small doses that are recommended as safe. Any loss of bone density in either men or women should be treated with calcium and drugs.

Facial appearance

As we get older our facial features change. There's a thinning of the hair, which is more marked in men. It often starts in the twenties, gathering pace and becoming particularly obvious by the time the man has reached fifty. Balding and the receding hairline over the temples is the result of diminished hormonal activity. It is a genetically influenced phenomenon. No amount of magic hair restorer or creams applied to the scalp is likely to restore one's hair to its original condition.

Provided the hair loss is not due to a disease, it usually affects only the hair on the head, leaving the hair on other parts of the body unchanged. There's no doubt that the male sex hormones play a role in triggering off this hair loss, although it hasn't been shown to be reversible by hormone treatment. Certainly, lack of hormone at an early age may accelerate the process, and, indeed, eunuchs tend to go bald early.

The process also occurs in women, but at a much slower pace. Women's hair tends to become thinner as they get older and the rate of its growth slows, resulting in longer and longer intervals between haircuts. The pubic hair of women also tends to thin and not infrequently it will tend to peak in the mid line (this is usually considered to be a characteristic of the male). These processes are slowed by HRT, although the hair will continue to thin slowly as the rate at which it grows continues to slow down in spite of hormone replacement. Greying is associated with changes in the structure and the content of the hair. It's an effect of ageing that tends to run in the family.

The skin

Skin ages because of the loss of elasticity in the subcutaneous tissues – those tissues beneath the skin. This causes the wrinkling and furrows that typify ageing. The skin also becomes thinner and tougher due to changes in the collagen tissue, of which it is composed. This gives it a weather-beaten look. While it is doubtful whether the loss of elasticity, which is the main cause of wrinkles, is influenced by exposure to the UV light in sunshine, there is good evidence that it hastens the changes that occur naturally in collagen. The brown spots that appear on the skin as one gets older are usually due to a fatty infiltration of the degenerating collagen. Thick, warty deposits, ungenerously termed 'senile keratomas' (or calluses), which often develop in the skin as we age, are often mistaken for skin tumours. If they are unsightly they can easily be removed by surgical excision.

It is important to realise that the loss of elasticity in the skin is irreversible and no amount of expensive creams with pseudoscientifically named ingredients can either stop or reverse the process. The effect of most of these 'junk' cosmetics is to cause water to be retained in the subcutaneous tissues, making them swell. This may conceal the wrinkle for a short time. The same effect is produced by sun-tanning.

Botox, a brand name of botulinum toxin, works in a different way. It causes a short-lived paralysis of the muscles that produce facial expression. The effect usually lasts from a few days to a month or two. Because the underlying muscle is paralysed, the frown or furrow becomes less obvious. The price paid is the loss of facial expression, giving the victim a somewhat dull and lifeless look.

There are two main giveaways of facial ageing. One is the furrow that runs between the corners of the nose and the ends of the lips, the nasolabial fold. It is this fold that is obliterated and smoothed out by surgical facelifts. The other is the development of loose skin under the eyes and the fatty infiltration in the upper eyelids. Together these give a sleepy, tired look to the face as we get older. They can be corrected by surgery.

A procedure called *blethroplasty* removes the bags under the eyes and the drooping-eyelid appearance, and a facelift will removed the excess sagging skin from the face, smoothing out the wrinkles and folds. Unless the facial changes associated with ageing are causing distress, we should accept them gracefully as part of the process of growing older rather than try to reverse what is essentially a natural process. For a few people in whom the effects of ageing are so exaggerated that they come to interfere with their lives, and in those whose careers depend on looking eternally young, surgery offers the only real opportunity to reverse the changes. It should only be undertaken by skilled, well-trained plastic surgeons. Like all operations, these procedures carry certain risks and the results are not always predictable or entirely satisfactory.

Activity

You only have to watch older people as they get out of their cars to realise that ageing imposes certain restrictions on one's activity. Unfortunately, however hard we exercise, it is impossible to maintain the same physical strength and the same stamina that we enjoyed when young. The combination of changes in the heart and lungs with the process of muscular degeneration and joint stiffness invariably takes its toll. It is necessary to anticipate this effect. To believe that there is some magic formula, or exercise regime, that will prevent the restriction in activity that occurs with age is to fool oneself.

Exercise

I recently saw a seventy-four-year-old man emerging from a health club, ashen white, doubled up with muscular pain, clutching his chest and pleading for a glass of water. This is the result of exercise mania. The belief that one can prevent the complex changes of age by exercise is nonsense. However much a seventy-year-old exercises, he will not become a Charles Atlas.

There is a common misconception that, if a little exercise is good for you (and certainly a sedentary lifestyle is bad for you), then a lot of exercise must be better. The body just does not work that way. Exercise should be taken like any medical treatment, in a dose that does maximum good; to overdose a patient can do positive harm.

The aim of exercise should be to minimise the loss of muscle tone, to maintain mobility of joints and to stretch the vertebral skeleton. This is best achieved by several short bursts of exercise rather than a single, prolonged strenuous bout of very vigorous exertion.

Deep-breathing exercises may help keep the remoter reaches of the lung aerated and increase the oxygenation of the blood. This is especially helpful following a lung infection. Similarly, a short bout of exercise that increases your pulse rate to about 120 a minute for 5 minutes may help to exercise the muscle of the heart.

To embark upon a new sport or activity that requires bouts of violent activity, especially if this associated with bending and twisting, is to invite physical problems. While, with training, we can increase our ability to engage in prolonged activity such as long-distance walking, it is rare to be able to train ourselves for anything greater than short bursts of vigorous physical effort. A healthy lifestyle should aim at trying to maintain as much joint flexibility as possible and to prevent any excessive loss of muscle power. In order to achieve this it is necessary to understand the changes that inevitably occur in the organs of the body as we get older.

Tiredness

Have you ever revisited a familiar scene from your youth and felt it impossible not to regret the loss of stamina and energy compared with what it was years ago? Hills you used to take in your stride now become a significant challenge. Whereas you could step out for three or four miles, you now become tired after a mile or two. Aches and pains in the joints often accompany the exhaustion caused by any attempt to repeat physical feats that were routine when you were younger.

This diminution in the reserve capacity for exercise, and the feeling of tiredness that results, is a very frequent complaint as we get older. Often it appears to come on suddenly, usually after an illness or period of debility. It seems as if we never quite recover from the tiredness we felt when unwell. In fact, it's a gradual phenomena associated with the effect of ageing upon the heart and lungs. While its effects can be deferred by regular exercise, there is an inevitability about its occurrence.

Physical tiredness should be distinguished from mental fatigue which may be the effect of sleepiness; a sign of insufficient stimulating activity or depression. Physical tiredness due to a lack of sleep is relatively rare if a person has had between six and eight hours sleep a day.

Body weight

Overweight used to be diagnosed by reference to average weight as given in the Metropolitan Life Assurance tables that were attached to weighing machines. The figures for the average weight were adjusted for both height and age. Today, with the body-mass index (BMI) being used to determine obesity, it is more difficult to see the way in which average weight increases steadily as we get older. Because the BMI uses the square of the height as the denominator, the effect of any diminution in stature results in an exaggerated increase in the BMI. It is unreasonable to label someone who has not had an increase in weight as obese merely because ageing has made them shorter.

How to calculate your BMI (body-mass index)

This measurement was originally proposed as a better index of actuarial life expectancy than the Metropolitan Life Assurance statistics that used to adorn weighing machines. It was proposed in 1980s by a Belgian epidemiologist, Adolph Quetelet. It used the surface area of the body (devised from a special formula – the Dubois formula) divided by the height in metres, squared. In the 1990s the body–surface area was replaced by the weight in kilograms so as to simplify the measurement. It was shown that actuarially any person with a BMI of 20 per cent or more above the average of 20 to 25 was at a greater risk of an early death.

Recently, separate BMIs have been calculated for adults and for children of various ages. There has only been a general agreement on these limits since about 2002 and they are generally accepted to be less valuable as a predictor of future ill health than has been suggested by the attention given them in the media.

The BMI is open to misunderstanding. Because of the exaggerated importance given to the measurement of height (it is the square of the height that is used), the inevitable loss of height that occurs as we get older tends to exaggerate the BMI. Thus, a loss of 0.05 metres (about 2 inches) causes the denominator to increase by 0.25, resulting in a significant change in the BMI. This error also distorts the BMI of pubescent children, since they (especially girls) vary considerably in their height at a given age, while their weight is largely unchanged.

It is generally recognised that it is the proportion of the body that is fat and its distribution within the body that determines the actual risk and that this is not necessarily revealed by the BMI.

Nevertheless, obesity can be a problem as we get older. It's a time when the calorific requirements of the body are decreasing because metabolic activity is slowing down. At the same time, the capacity for physical exertion and exercise is reduced, further reducing the need for food. Unless there is a simultaneous reduction in appetite, we tend to put on weight. Many people find that their capacity to eat three full meals a day is lessened as they get older and that the craving for large protein meals is decreased. This would appear to be nature's way of adapting to the changes brought about by ageing.

Obesity is often associated with a propensity to diabetes in this age group, which makes it sensible to keep your weight under control. Excess weight also imposes an extra burden on muscles and joints and on the heart at the very time that their efficiency is decreasing.

There's a definite correlation between a decreased life expectancy and excessive weight (20 per cent above the maximum BMI for your age and height). A similar reduction in life expectancy can also be demonstrated in those who are more than 10 per cent underweight. Dieting to the point of skinniness should be avoided, since it is as dangerous to be too thin as too fat.

We'll look at obesity in more detail in Chapter 13, 'Weighty Matters'.

'For God's sake swallow your pride and stop
wearing out my carpet.'

Chapter Six

Ageing and the Brain and Heart

The brain

One of the first signs of the ageing of the brain is loss of memory. The sudden failure to remember the name of someone you met only a few days ago or the contents of the book you read last month comes a shock At first it is possible to regard this as a temporary lapse brought on by tiredness or emotion, but when it starts to happen with increasing frequency, as it invariably does, it has to be accepted that something is happening in one's brain.

This change is commonly referred to in the media as *Alzheimer's disease*. However, this is incorrect: the German neurologist Alois Alzheimer (1864–1915) described *premature* mental senility, and the term should be strictly reserved for pre-senile dementia. The pathology of true Alzheimer's disease and its ultimate progression is very different from what occurs with ageing.

Memory failure in the elderly typically starts with the loss of memory for recent events, while a detailed recollection of long-past happenings is maintained. It is the realisation that it is possible to remember, in perfect detail, an event that happened twenty years ago while not being able to recall the name of the film one saw last week that makes one aware of the deterioration that is occurring.

The next stage usually involves the inability to remember names and titles: *nominal aphasia*. The victim soon learns to prevaricate until someone else proffers the forgotten name, or to avoid having to use the name by describing the person's relationship to someone whose name *can* be remembered. It is this difficulty in reaching for information that has been stored in the deeper recesses of the brain that causes people to think that they are becoming senile. It is important to realise that these changes are inevitable and common and they are not the beginnings of senility. They do not affect mental acuity, deductive capacity or the ability to make sensible and rational decisions, although they may slow down the response to an emergency situation. We have only to see the difference in the time it takes for an older person to find the answer to a question in a panel game to realise that access to our memory bank of knowledge takes longer and is more difficult as we get older.

A defective memory is made worse by tiredness, depression, alcohol and sedative drugs such as Valium. If ever you find yourself having to make any public presentation, it is sensible to wait till you've made it before taking alcohol. Before making any verbal presentation, make a note of key phrases, names and places.

It has been suggested that our memory can be kept in better shape by mental exercises such as taking part in word games, Sudoku and crossword puzzles. While this may have a limited beneficial effect, it is doubtful whether any mental exercises can be relied upon, in the long term, to prevent the inevitable mental changes of ageing. There is no doubt that repeatedly using a name reinforces it in one's memory and helps one to recall it at a future time. The mental deterioration that occurs with age undoubtedly gets worse more quickly in those who lead a solitary life.

It is not uncommon for people to avoid unnecessary social contact for fear of revealing the failings of their memory. This can become a self-perpetuating disaster. Without the stimulation of friends and interesting conversation, the memory will deteriorate rapidly to a point where any conversation becomes very dull and restricted. It has been suggested that we should seek regular *mental* stimulation in the same way we indulge in *physical* exercise. This would seem to be sensible advice. Whenever possible, it should be combined with discussions and debate where words and experiences are recalled in order to express opinions. This reinforces the scope of our vocabulary and helps us to access our memory bank.

The deterioration in the brain's control over the body can be demonstrated by trying to stand on one leg. This effect becomes obvious when the act of putting on trousers or socks can be achieved only by holding on to a support. Young people can stand on one leg for many minutes, but it becomes increasingly difficult as we get older. The development of a shaky tremor of the outstretched hand commonly occurs in older people. These tremors become evident if the arms are extended stiffly at right angles to the body. Tremors usually become less obvious if a weighty object is held in the hand. They are common sign of ageing and don't necessarily herald the onset of Parkinson's disease.

The principle cause of these changes is a slowing in the rate of production of the chemical messengers, or transmitters, that the brain cells use to communicate with each other and to send their commands down the nerves to the rest of the body. It is these transmitter chemicals that access the memory stores in the brain. Although drugs are available that prolong the action of some of the chemical messengers, they are not specific and don't act solely on the particular areas of the brain involved in memory. They increase the amount of chemical messenger available at all the sites where they are released. As a result, these drugs are given in a low dose so as to prevent unpleasant and dangerous side effects, such as tremors, anxiety and convulsions. Considerable pharmaceutical interest and effort is being directed at finding a 'magic bullet' drug that will selectively target the areas of the brain associated with memory.

In view of the inevitable deterioration in memory as we get older, it is sensible not to become involved in pursuits that put a premium on memory. Further-education classes that necessitate committing a lot of facts to memory should be avoided. Because of the deterioration in memory, it's a good idea to use an *aide-mémoire* whenever possible to assist in remembering dates, appointments and other obligations. The problem of many of the more sophisticated electronic devices that are available is that, unless they are used constantly, it becomes harder as we get older to remember how to access their information!

Dizziness and fainting

Dizziness and fainting are common complaints as one gets older. They are nearly always caused by a sudden drop in the blood supply to the brain. This is most usually the result of a failure of the nervous system to make the automatic adjustments necessary to compensate for a change in posture, from a sitting or lying position to standing up. When such a change of posture takes place the brain sends messages to the heart and the blood vessels, causing the heart to pump more blood, and the blood vessels, especially the in the gut and the legs, to constrict.

The combined effect of these changes is to keep up the supply of blood to the brain, where it is essential, at the expense of the various less essential structures. If these compensatory mechanisms fail, blood tends to pool in the legs and gut, causing a reduction in the amount available to be pumped to the brain.

These symptoms become more prevalent in the elderly because of the general slowdown in the rate of response by the brain due to a reduction in the production of transmitter chemicals as we get older. Other factors that may magnify this effect include:

- the hardening of the blood vessels that occurs as part of the ageing process, making them less responsive

- medication for high blood pressure that may interfere with the nervous control of the blood vessels
- a heavy meal that diverts blood to the gut
- a hot environment which promotes blood flow to the skin

Knowing why and when these symptoms can occur may help us to take precautions to avoid them.

There are other causes of dizziness and fainting, some of which require medical intervention. Dizziness may be caused by an interference with the ability of the heart to increase its pumping rate, in spite of receiving the signals from the brain. This is usually caused by some degree of block in the nervous conducting system contained within the heart. Heart block often shows itself as bouts of fainting. It can usually be treated satisfactorily by means of a cardiac pacemaker.

Deficient sugar in the blood will cause dizziness. Although this condition can occur spontaneously, it is more likely to follow an inappropriate dose of insulin.

Occasionally, one of the two main arteries to the head may become narrowed. In this case the other artery becomes the dominant means of providing the brain with oxygen and nutriment. Sharply turning the head to one side may constrict the good artery, causing you to feel faint. This condition is responsive to surgery.

Blood pressure

Any reading of blood pressure is given as two numbers, the higher (the systolic) pressure and the lower (or diastolic) pressure. A normal, young, healthy, resting adult should have a blood pressure of 120 (systolic) over about 80 (diastolic) pressure. The pressures are measured against the column of mercury that they would support. Thus, a systolic blood pressure of 120 would push a column of mercury up to a height of 120 millimetres.

The difference between these two pressures is called the *pulse pressure*; it causes the pulse wave that can be felt at the wrist. A feeble pulse at the wrist suggests that a small amount of blood is being pumped out at each beat of the heart.

As the height of both of these pressures is determined by different factors, both are of diagnostic and prognostic significance. The systolic pressure reflects the pumping power of the heart and the distensibilty of the major blood vessels, while the diastolic pressure largely reflects the rate at which the blood pumped into the aorta can escape, either through the arterioles of the vascular bed or back into the heart in the case of a leaky valve.

The progressive loss of elastic tissue in the aorta and the major blood vessels and its replacement by non-elastic fibrous tissue leads to a rise in blood pressure. While it has been suggested that high blood pressure is due to too much dietary salt, this is unlikely to be its primary cause in most people. A high salt intake may cause water retention and a short-lived rise in blood pressure but this will occur only if the usual hugely distensible capacity of the circulation is restricted by a hardening of the arteries. In most instances the effect will be minimal.

By far the most important factors in the rise in blood pressure that occurs as we get older are the mechanical changes caused by the hardening of the blood vessels.

In a young person when the heart contracts and squirts out its content of blood much of the energy is dissipated in stretching the wall of the aorta. The stretched aorta, like a stretched piece of elastic, now has the potential energy to contract slowly and squeeze the blood around the vessels of the body. The peak of the pressure reached in the aorta is said to be *damped down* by the elasticity of the aorta and other major vessels. As we get older and the elastic tissue is progressively replaced by fibrous tissue, the walls of the aorta and great vessels come to resemble rigid pipes rather than elastic tubes. When the heart contracts, it now forces its contents into the rigid pipelike aorta. All the energy created by the contraction of the heart now becomes turned into a giant pressure wave. The pressure reached at the peak of the heart's contraction in an older person is much higher than it is in a young person who has plenty of elasticity in the main blood vessels. This is the principal cause of the increase in the peak – or *systolic* – blood pressure as we get older.

The increased rigidity of the vascular system of the older person also affects the smaller blood vessels, the *arterioles*. Rigidity of these vessels prevents the ready 'run-off' of blood from the ends of the arteries. This tends to maintain the pressure in the system between heartbeats at a higher level than in a younger person with more distensible arterioles. This may cause a rise in the *diastolic* blood pressure.

Taking the pressure

Doctors use an instrument called a *sphygmo-manometer* to measure blood pressure. That's quite a mouthful! Sphyg comes from a Greek word meaning pulsation. A *manometer* is an instrument for measuring pressure. You've probably had that inflatable cuff put around your arm, which tightens, restricting blood flow, and watched the doctor reading from the mercury column.

This device requires the doctor to use a

stethoscope to listen to the brachial artery (the one near the elbow). The cuff's pressure is gradually released, and the examiner is able to hear a whooshing sound as the blood begins to circulate again. The pressure at which this begins is the *systolic* blood pressure (systolic describes the contraction of the heart). The cuff is relaxed further until this sound can no longer be heard. The pressure at that point is the diastolic blood pressure (*diastolic* describes the expansion of the heart).

Sometimes, doctors will wish to know your *ambulatory* blood pressure: this involves measuring it for 24 hours as you go about your daily business, using a portable device.

High blood pressure is sometimes called the 'silent killer' because in many cases you're unlikely to know you've got it, so it's as well to have it checked regularly. The reading you will get is the systolic figure over the diastolic figure (e.g. 120 over 90). Readings will differ according to age and other factors, although there will be an optimum your doctor will recommend you aim for.

High blood pressure – also known as *hypertension* – is a considerable health-risk factor. Since drugs became available to reduce high blood pressure, the incidence of strokes has decreased by between 20 and 30 per cent. It is one of the great success stories of modern medicine. Because of the importance of controlling blood pressure, GPs are encouraged to test patients on a regular basis. Unfortunately, while the objective is laudable, it is quite difficult to interpret a patient's blood pressure from a single reading taken, on one occasion. Ideally, the patient should be rested and relaxed, and the pressure should be read in both arms in the recumbent and erect positions. The significance of a single high reading should be questioned if the pulse rate is also raised, as it suggests the patient was not truly at rest.

The cause of a high reading should be assessed by looking for evidence of its effect on the heart. Persistent high blood pressure usually causes cardiac enlargement. This can be detected either by physical examination of the chest or by an ECG (electrocardiogram) examination. The danger of reducing the blood pressure in a patient who does not have established hypertension is greater than that of not treating a patient with only a modestly raised pressure. There are reports of patients, who have been prescribed drugs to lower their blood pressure – who probably did not require treatment – feeling dizzy after meals, fainting on standing up and in one case of passing out while driving a car.

A persistently high blood pressure, especially the diastolic pressure, increases the work of the heart, which has to achieve a higher pressure in order to eject blood against an increased resistance. It imposes an 'after-load' on the heart. As one gets older the ability of the heart to work harder becomes more and more limited. The increase in the workload imposed by high blood pressure may be the last straw that pushes it into failure. The kidneys are also susceptible to the effect of sustained high blood pressure and they may undergo irreversible damage, but the greatest risk in the elderly is that of a stroke due to the rupture of a small stiff artery in the brain.

There are three types of stroke. The first, which is usually called 'a young person's stroke', is due to a rupture of a congenitally weak part of a blood vessel in the brain. The other two, both of which are associated with high blood pressure or pressures that fluctuate wildly, are caused either by a rupture or a blockage of a blood vessel in the brain. It is important to diagnose which type of stroke has taken place as soon as possible. This can be done with an MRI (magnetic resonance imaging) scan. A cerebral thrombosis should be treated by the immediate use of clot-busting drugs while a cerebral haemorrhage needs to be treated by controlling the blood pressure.

The drugs available for the treatment of high blood pressure vary in the way they work. GPs are advised to use those drugs that are statistically most effective in the greatest number of patients, the so-called 'best practice'. While this benefits most patients in the majority of cases, it causes significant side effects in a few. It would be preferable if doctors were able to find out the likely cause of the hypertension before they chose the drug regime so that they could select one most likely to suit each particular patient best.

The first effective treatment of high blood pressure was by means of beta-blocking drugs, which counteract some of the actions of adrenalin on the heart and blood vessels. They are still widely used for those people who react to anxiety by becoming excessively agitated. This causes an increase in their heart rate as well as their blood pressure. The beta blockers have been largely superseded by more specific drugs with fewer effects on other bodily systems.

Calcium-blocking drugs, often combined with a diuretic, affect the contractile efficiency of the small arterioles, reducing the resistance to blood flow in these vessels and reducing the lowest, or diastolic, pressure. The third group of drugs blocks the activity of the angiotensin hormone, which also acts to constrict the smaller blood vessels. Angiotensin is produced as a result of a fall in the amount of blood flowing throughout the kidney. The amount of angiotensin produced has been found to be increased in those on a very low-salt diet.

The emphasis placed on reducing high blood pressure in the National Health Service is justified by the expectation that the incidence of strokes and cardiac failure can be reduced still further. The proven efficacy of the drugs available for the treatment of high blood pressure makes any possible benefit from a severe reduction in salt intake of only marginal potential benefit. This is especially true in the elderly, who are particularly susceptible to heat stroke and dehydration if they become salt-deficient.

There is some evidence that a persistent high blood pressure may cause a constriction of the blood vessels supplying the brain, starving it of blood, and this may contribute to some of the memory loss that occurs with ageing.

The heart

Like all the muscles of the body, the muscle of the heart becomes less efficient with age. Muscle tissue becomes stiff and fibrous and deposits of fat infiltrate between its cells. As a result it is unable to increase its performance to meet a sudden demand as well as that of a young person. In a young person the heart responds to exercise or stress, by both increasing the amount of blood it pumps out with each beat and by increasing the rate at which it contracts.

Fit young people may be able to double their output per beat, but this becomes more and more difficult as they get older. It is commonly found that patients over sixty-five can increase the volume pumped by only 15–20 per cent. As a result, if the same demand is made on an older person the heart has to make up for this lack of reserve capacity by increasing the rate at which it pumps. A sudden bout of exercise or an emotional strain may result in a precipitous increase in heart rate in older people. This is one of the principal causes of angina, the crushing chest pain that occurs on exertion.

To understand why an increase in the heart rate causes angina, we have to consider how the normal heart is supplied with blood. The cells lining the inside of the heart are very sensitive to a lack of oxygen. Oxygen normally reaches these cells from the blood carried in the vessels that lie on the outside of the heart, the *coronary arteries*. These vessels have to penetrate the thick muscular wall of the heart to reach the cells lining its interior. When the heart contracts these vessels are squashed and closed. They can supply blood to the inside of the heart only during the time, between beats, when the heart is relaxed. The faster the heart beats, the less time it spends in a relaxed state and therefore the shorter the time for blood to supply the cells of the heart's lining. The resultant reduction in oxygen supply causes the pain of angina. Angina is especially likely to occur if the coronary arteries are narrowed by atheromatous plaques (basically, atheromas are fatty deposits in an artery).

The treatment of this condition depends on treating any major blockage of the blood vessels supplying the heart and limiting any increase in heart rate. Coronary artery dilatation – by angioplasty, a stent (a tubular structure for keeping bodily tubes open) or surgical replacement of a blocked artery – ensures that as much blood is available as possible to supply the heart. Beta blockers, and other drugs that limit any possible increase in the heart rate, give the vessels penetrating the heart sufficient time between contractions to supply the sensitive cells lining the heart with oxygen.

Like all muscles, if the heart is not exercised it will deteriorate. This is why you should try to exert yourself vigorously, so as to put up your heart rate to over a hundred beats per minute for five to ten minutes, at least once a day. Care should be taken not to exercise to the point of angina, or for longer than ten minutes, and to rest for an equal time after the exertion, to allow the heart muscle to recover.

Cholesterol and heart disease

Ever since it was found that patients with a high blood cholesterol level were at a much increased risk of a heart attack, there has been an assumption that it is the high level of cholesterol in the blood that causes the atheromatous plaques that bring on heart attacks. It was then a short jump of reasoning that put the blame for the high blood cholesterol on an excessive intake of dietary fat. This supposition was supported by the finding that countries with a high dietary fat intake, such as Finland, had a high incidence of heart disease. This assertion was not unreasonable, since atheromas are largely composed

CHEMICAL FORMULA

FOR CHOLESTEROL

of cholesterol. To combat this, diets that were low in fats, especially those so-called bad fats, the saturated ones that are raised when the blood cholesterol level rises after a fatty meal, were widely advocated.

This view is now seriously challenged and is almost certainly wrong. It has been demonstrated, in large prospective trials, that, while diet may reduce blood cholesterol in the short term, it does not do so over any prolonged period. By including more countries in the study of the effect of a high fat intake on the incidence of heart disease, it has been found that there is no correlation between the amount of fat consumed by a population and the incidence of heart attacks.

The most serious doubt about this proposed relationship is the knowledge that the cholesterol deposited in atheromatous plaques does not come from food but is manufactured in the liver and the wall of the artery by specific enzyme activity which is blocked by statins (we met these drugs in Chapter 4). It remains true that those with a serum cholesterol level over 6mg per 100ml have a statistically greater risk of a heart attack and a shorter expectation of life than those whose cholesterol level is 4.5–6mg per 100ml. It is also found that a blood cholesterol lower than 3mg per 100ml is potentially dangerous and is associated with a raised mortality rate. It is now generally accepted that there is little reason to restrict a normal, reasonable intake of dietary fats and that the advantages of unsaturated fat over saturated fat have been exaggerated.

Cholesterol and statins

Cholesterol is a steroid, a complex fatty molecule that consists of five boxlike rings of molecules joined along common sides.

It is an essential part of our body. It forms a major part of the membrane around every cell and is especially important in those areas of the cell wall that allow the passage of essential chemicals into and out of the cell.

It is found in high concentration in the brain, liver and prostate gland. It is formed when a tissue degenerates or a blood clot is absorbed. Like other steroids, such as the sex hormones and cortisone, it is manufactured by an enzyme system whose activity seems to be controlled by a feedback system. Thus, if the level falls, more steroid is produced and vice versa.

In the case of cholesterol, more than 90 per cent of that found in the blood is manufactured in our livers. Any cholesterol that is taken in as food, for example with eggs or shellfish, is treated as a foreign substance by the liver and is almost entirely broken down into its constituent molecules. Eating food rich in cholesterol may temporally increase the blood level, but over any significant period the actual cholesterol level in the blood will be set by the activity of the enzymes in the liver. It is the cholesterol produced locally and by the liver that causes the deposits in the atheromatous plaques in the arteries.

Actuarial statistics confirm that those with a high level of blood cholesterol are at a greater risk of having a heart attack. This effect is largely overcome if the cholesterol level is reduced. A blood cholesterol level of 4.5 to 5.5 millimoles per litre is considered satisfactory. A level lower than 4.5 is associated with non-cardiac problems.

Those with a blood cholesterol level that is consistently above 6 should take one of the statin drugs to lower the amount of cholesterol in the blood. These drugs work by blocking the enzyme that produces the complex five-box structure from a string of molecules. Too much statin will produce muscle pains and in a large excess may affect liver function in susceptible individuals. The statistical benefits of a reduction in the incidence of heart attacks following the introduction of statins become apparent only after two to three years.

The place of the statin drugs in this story is important. These drugs interfere with the enzyme system that is required for the formation of cholesterol in the body. By preventing its formation in the liver, it reduces blood cholesterol levels, and by interfering with the formation of cholesterol in blood vessels, it prevents atheromatous plaques forming in the blood vessels. There is good evidence, which becomes apparent after about three years of taking statins, that their use reduces the rate of heart attacks and increases longevity.

The use of low doses (75mg) of aspirin each day has a small but significant effect on the incidence of heart attacks. The studies of the effect of low-dose aspirin have suggested that it is most useful in those in whom there is a special risk factor, such as a family history of heart attacks, and those who have already had an attack. It slightly increases the risk of haemorrhagic strokes while reducing the number of strokes due to a thrombosis. It acts by reducing the stickiness of the platelets, an effect it shares with the anti-inflammatory drugs.

One of the puzzling facts that defy a rational explanation is that all over the world the incidence of heart attacks, which suddenly increased after 1950, is decreasing from the peak incidence reached in 1960 to 1980, in spite of the increasing age of the population. It would be nice to be able to claim that this was the effect of modern medicine and better diet, but this is not supported by any evidence. Indeed, in countries where the effect is most marked, such as Canada, there has been an increase in the average daily consumption of dietary fats.

Chapter Seven

Other Effects of Ageing

Bones and joints

As we get older, the joints become stiffer and start to ache. No longer can we leap out of bed in the morning and touch our toes. Getting out of bed is followed by a period of stretching and straightening. When we try to put our socks on, our toes seem to be getting further and further from our body as bending our back becomes more and more difficult. While some fortunate individuals manage to put off these effects until they are over seventy, for most, they start to become obvious at about sixty. It is important to understand the changes that are occurring in the body that cause these effects and what measures may help to minimise their impact.

The slow loss of elastic tissue coupled with the degeneration of collagen and its replacement by stiff, unyielding fibrous tissue starts when we reach only forty or fifty and continues relentlessly as we get older. These changes restrict the range of movements possible in joints. In some joints the reduction in the range of possible movements is very small, but the sum of the effects in all the joints leads to an overall pattern of stiffness and rigidity.

Because of the unyielding nature of fibrous tissue, vigorous movements easily tear the tendons and capsules around the joints. This makes them vulnerable to tendonitis, strains and 'frozen' or painful joint syndromes. Tennis elbow, frozen shoulder, painful thumbs and acute back pain become increasingly prevalent, especially following unaccustomed exercise.

Many of these tears take weeks or months to recover, during which time we're likely to besiege the doctor's surgery seeking a cure. This often results in unnecessary X-rays and injections of local anaesthetics and cortisone. Most of these treatments give no more than transient relief. Fibrous tissue heals very slowly, because it has a poor blood supply; an injection is unlikely to hurry this process. Opinion is divided as to whether gentle exercise or complete rest is preferable; it probably makes no difference to the slow but certain recovery. Anti-inflammatory drugs may help to reduce the pain and swelling.

In the elderly and in those on long-term corticosteroid treatment, tendons may become thinned and weakened so that they rupture. This is especially true of the Achilles' tendon in the heel. It is a very painful condition and usually requires surgical treatment.

Arthritis

It is important to distinguish between the gradual wearing-out process that affects the joint surfaces of the major weight-bearing joints such as the knee and the hip, which causes osteoarthritis, and rheumatoid arthritis, which affects the soft tissues around the joint.

Rheumatoid arthritis affects the joints of younger people, especially the finger joints of menopausal women, although it can occur in all joints in all age groups. It is often an allergic type of response by the body to an infection or to psoriasis. In its most fulminating form it causes a painful destruction of the joint.

The pain and swelling of rheumatoid arthritis is different from those of osteoarthritis, which usually occurs in an older age group or after an injury that involved the joint. The pain of osteoarthritis is made worse by movement. It can usually be controlled by anti inflammatory drugs, by gentle exercises that maintain the tone of the muscles around the joint and by losing any excess weight. Ultimately, if the pain in the joint interferes with an active lifestyle, the joint should be replaced. Since no artificial joint is quite as good as the original, and they survive less well if subjected to the sort of vigorous pounding from the exertions likely to be indulged in by a younger person, the replacement should be delayed as long as possible.

Rheumatoid arthritis requires medical treatment with anti-inflammatory drugs, rest and cortisone. As the inflammatory response that underlies this condition tends to decrease with age, rheumatoid arthritis becomes less painful as we get older. Unfortunately, the joint destruction that it causes remains and often reduces the usefulness of the affected joint.

Back pain

Back pain is common as we get older; indeed, complete freedom from backache is unusual. It is helpful and reassuring to distinguish acute back strain from that of a slipped disc, where the pressure on a nerve may cause pain radiating down the leg – sciatica. If you lie on your back on a hard surface and raise one outstretched leg at a time, and can't raise it more than thirty degrees without severe back pain, this suggests nerve involvement due to a slipped disc.

Both conditions are usually initiated by lifting a heavy weight, especially if this is attempted when the trunk is twisted. The pain of both conditions commonly starts in the small of the back. Both should be treated in the first instance by rest on your back, warmth and anti-inflammatory drugs.

There is general agreement that, provided there are no shooting pains preventing you from raising the straightened leg while lying on your back, gentle mobilisation should be encouraged after twelve to twenty-four hours. If there are shooting pains into the thigh or down the leg, longer rest may be necessary. Should the sciatica persist, if circulatory changes such as cold blue toes occur or muscle weakness becomes apparent in the legs, it is best to get some medical advice.

Although all severe unremitting back pain that doesn't respond to rest should be investigated (there are some causes of backache that are not due to the backbone), an operation on the back should be considered as a last resort, unless there is evidence of progressive nerve damage.

Osteoporosis

Osteoporosis is a disease of ageing. Its effects are genetically linked and vary from person to person. Softening of the bone results from tipping the normal fine balance between the new bone formation and absorption of the existing bone, in favour of its absorption. The natural balance depends on several factors: the type of bone, the parathyroid activity, vitamin D, sex hormone and exercise.

There are two types of bone in the body: membrane bone and cartilaginous bone. Membrane bone is the evolutionary derivative of the scales of fish and the shell skeleton of turtles and reptiles. Cartilage bone develops, as its name suggests, in structures that start the evolutionary trail as a cartilaginous support for vulnerable body structures. In general, the membrane bones, such as the skull, get heavier as we get older, whereas the cartilage bones suffer a loss of calcium and osteoporosis.

Osteoporosis is more evident in postmenopausal women than in men. It affects the vertebrae, causing them to become wedged or collapsed, and the long bones of the thigh and arm, causing them to become vulnerable to injury. The loss of calcium in the thigh bone increases the risk of it breaking after a fairly trivial trip and fall. It used to be commonplace to treat one or two elderly patients with fractured hips most nights in hospital emergency rooms.

Hormone-replacement therapy has dramatically reduced the risk of osteoporosis in women. Unfortunately, no such remedy is available for men, principally due to the possibility of an increased risk of cancer of the prostate. Other therapies that stimulate calcium deposition are available but for them to be effective it is necessary to combine them with active exercise and to start them as early as possible. There is good evidence that a sedentary life leads to an increased rate of decalcification in bones.

Exercise is extremely important in the prevention of joint stiffness and pain. It's necessary if we're to maintain a full range of movements in all our joints for as long as possible. Gentle swimming and stretching are ideal. Prolonged vigorous exercise may do more harm than good. It's better to perform simple stretching exercises two or three times a day rather than a single burst of strenuous activity.

Too often an unfit, untrained person suddenly decides to lose weight or to 'get fit' and embarks on a crash course of vigorous exercises such as jogging, squash or weightlifting. This frequently ends in disaster as that person gets older. It can cause stress fractures, joint disease, torn ligaments and heart failure. There are extravagant claims that exercise can prevent cancer, cure asthma and prolong life. None of these assertions has a significant body of scientific support; indeed, it would difficult to postulate a mechanism by which it might be brought about. There is good evidence that exercise is associated with the production of endorphins, nature's own happy pill.

Sport and exercise should be taken in the correct dose, like any other treatment. Too much can cause harm. Indeed, if vigorous sports were without any deleterious side effects there would be no need for the sports-injury clinics treating the painful and often permanent bone injuries that can occur.

There is good evidence that a sedentary lifestyle shortens life expectancy. It is therefore recommended that one should exercise regularly. This can take the form of a really brisk walk of about one to two miles a day, or a shorter period of a programmed exercise that moves all the joints, energetically, through a full range of movements. Ambling around a shop is not good exercise. Many household chores, such as ironing and sweeping, are surprisingly effective as a form of exercise. The object of exercise is to maintain mobility and to prevent degeneration of muscle. Muscle-building regimes are doomed to failure in the over-fifties, since within a few years they lead to an increase in the rate of fatty degeneration and atrophy of the hypertrophied muscle cells.

Sleep

Studies carried out in dark rooms and sleep laboratories suggest that most people, left in a dark, completely nonstimulating environment, enjoy about eight hours' sleep a day. This usually occurs as one period of about six hours and another, about twelve hours later, of one or two hours. It would appear that, left entirely to our own devices, we would naturally cat-nap after lunch.

As we get older, it is common for the pattern of sleep to become less regular. It is not uncommon to have some nights when we wake in the early hours and others when we have difficulty in going to sleep. This is especially true in wintertime. Sometimes it is a response to an irregular lifestyle, the need to empty the bladder more frequently or a pressing problem; not infrequently, it is due to a feeling of anticlimax following some important event or to depression. Occasional sleepless nights should not be considered abnormal or a reason to resort to sleeping pills. However, a prolonged bout of disturbed nights can seriously interfere with our enjoyment of life.

Restless-leg syndrome

This syndrome has been recognised only in the last twenty or so years. Before that the occurrence of the restless leg, a compulsion to move, bend and stretch the leg, was considered an idiosyncratic response to tiredness. It is now recognised as a syndrome with its effects occurring with increasing frequency as one gets older, especially over the age of forty-five. It usually occurs soon after one goes to bed and is a common cause of sleeplessness. The cause of the symptom is unknown but it could be related to the slow degenerative changes that occur in the muscle or nerve at rest. It can sometimes be relieved by a small dose of a dopamine-like drug Mirapexin (primipexole). Since drug treatment is not without complications, it should be used only when the syndrome occurs regularly. Unless it occurs very frequently it should either be tolerated or a sleeping pill used to help overcome the effect of the condition.

An insomniac often dreads going to bed for fear of lying awake, tossing and turning. An active day with plenty of physical exercise may overcome a temporary problem. A regular time of retiring and a drink of warm milk or chocolate at night might help to encourage sleep. There's good evidence that the pattern of dark nights and sunny days helps to imprint the sleep pattern in the brain through the secretion of melatonin during the hours of darkness. Most people sleep better during the summer months.

Sleeping pills are useful, but they should be reserved for those times when some event has provoked a temporary disturbance of sleep, such as the effect of jet lag, a bereavement or unexpected bad news. They should not be used indiscriminately. When they are used they should be taken in an effective dose for as short a period as possible. They should not be used for more than two or three days at a time.

The danger is that a few people become dependent on sleeping pills, fearing a night of torture, tossing and turning while the hours pass by. Sleeping pills should be regarded as a temporary prop to overcome a specific sleeping problem, not a long-term solution.

Although some people swear that alcohol keeps them awake, the evidence is to the contrary: a glass of alcohol before bed can help reduce the anxieties that keep people awake at night. The effect of caffeine is less clear. Undoubtedly, caffeine keeps the mind buzzing, but the blood level required for this effect is far greater than that found in the blood of the *occasional* coffee or tea drinker. It is possible to achieve such a level if tea or coffee is drunk in commercial quantities or several cups are drunk within a few hours of going to bed. In experimental conditions, complete quietness predisposes to sleepiness but few can achieve this in real life. A radio or audio tape story at bedtime, especially if played quietly, can distract attention from other environmental sounds, lessening their effect and helping to promote sleep.

There undoubtedly are people who manage to go through life with less than six hours of sleep a night, but laboratory studies have suggested that those who claim to sleep for only three or four hours a night cat-nap during the day, although they may be unaware of doing so.

It would seem, from dark-room studies, that there is a physiological urge to nap after lunch. This behavioural pattern is common in Mediterranean countries and has a sound physiological basis. As you get older and the opportunity presents itself, it's a habit that should be encouraged. It allows you to enjoy longer evenings without feeling sleepy and to worry less about the occasional disturbed night's sleep.

Eating and drinking

As we get older we inevitably become less physically active and need fewer calories to support our lifestyle. The reduction, while real, is less than we might anticipate, since much of the food we eat is used in maintaining our body temperature. Unless there is some reduction in the amount of food eaten, we inevitably put on weight. Middle-aged obesity is the result.

Although an increase in exercise can ratchet up our metabolism a little, the only real answer is to cut down on the amount of food eaten. This is helped by the slowing of all metabolic processes, including those of digestion and appetite.

Gastric emptying becomes slower as we age, contributing to a feeling of fullness after meals. If you bolt down your food, it's more likely that it will leave a feeling of discomfort accompanied by dizziness and faintness, especially if you get up from the table to indulge in physical exertion of any sort. It is sensible to sit at the table for several minutes after the end of a large meal to allow the stomach to empty.

It is not uncommon for intolerance to certain foods to develop as we get older. Fried food, onions, peppers and garlic often cause indigestion and it is not unusual for a so-called 'food allergy' to develop. Most of these are merely expressions of the slowdown in the metabolic processing of a particular food substance. This is especially true of fatty foods.

People frequently develop sensitivity to red wine, finding it gives them a hangover and headaches. This is possibly due to the higher content of aldehydes and ketones, which are found in immature red wines compared with white ones. These typically cause a dry mouth and headache some hours after the wine has been drunk. In some cases it causes a headache after you take a drink of water the following day.

Because of the slowdown in the metabolic process, foods are metabolised more slowly in the liver, once they are absorbed from the gut and enter the bloodstream. Alcohol takes longer to be detoxified and may take longer to be cleared from the bloodstream. Working against this effect is the process known as *enzyme induction*, in which previous exposure to a chemical, such as alcohol, induces a speeding up of the ability to detoxify any compound with a similar chemical structure.

The body requires 2–3 litres of fluid a day in order to excrete the waste products of metabolism in the urine and to meet the water lost during breathing and sweating. Increasing the fluid intake beyond this level merely causes more frequent trips to the toilet. It does not increase the rate of detoxification. In mammals, the liver plays the main role in rendering potentially toxic substances harmless and in a form in which they can be excreted by the kidneys. Increasing the fluid intake does not increase the rate of this metabolic process.

As we get older, the kidneys lose some of their ability to concentrate the urine by reabsorbing water. To make up for this it is sensible to drink more fluid, especially in hot weather and after exercise. Of the 2–3 litres of fluid required, at least half will inevitably be taken in as food. Fruit, vegetables and fish have a large water content. Of the total fluid requirement, about 1 litre should be taken as a liquid. It doesn't mater whether this is water, fruit juice, tea or beer. It doesn't have to be in the form of expensive bottled water, either. The body has an exquisitely sensitive mechanism for notifying us of the need for water: it is called thirst. The drinking of extra fluid beyond satiation of thirst is unnecessary.

In abnormally hot weather or after vigorous exercise, the body keeps cool by sweating, which causes a loss of salt and water. In those used to the heat, the body adapts and conserves salt, minimising the amount lost in this way. This control mechanism becomes less effective as we get older. While we become aware of the loss of water through thirst, we are often unaware of the shortage of salt. Under these circumstances a high salt intake is essential for life. There is little doubt that many of the elderly people who die in heat waves do so because of venous thrombosis and strokes due to dehydration caused by salt deficiency. The present campaign against eating salt could result in the loss of the ability to keep the body cool in hot weather and to an increased risk of cerebral thrombosis.

Eyes and ears

Our eyesight diminishes as we get older. It becomes evident when we notice an inability to read the small print in a telephone directory or to see distant objects, such as car number plates, clearly. It is caused by a loss of elasticity in the thin transparent covering of the lens.

A similar degenerative process is responsible for the formation of cataracts within the lens. Whenever possible, a lens extraction for the removal of a cataract should be accompanied by an implant of an artificial lens. Although this not as good as a normal lens, it does offer significant compensation for the visual loss. Even more importantly, it offers some protection against retinal prolapse by creating a buffer between the two chambers of the eye.

A deterioration in hearing is very common as we get older. This can be overcome by the use of simple small hearing aids. Probably the commonest cause of hearing difficulty in older people is their reluctance to accept that they have a hearing problem and their refusal to use these aids. It is common for older people to blame their spouse for mumbling, or speaking too softly, rather than to admit they are getting hard of hearing.

'I'm awfully sorry dear, but I may have to forego a night of unbridled passion in favour of double chocolate fudge cake.'

Chapter Eight

Sex in the Third Age

As I'm sure you've gathered by now, as we get older, the workings of our bodies become slower. This is especially true for the parts of the cell, the *mitochondria*, that manufacture the enzymes and secretions that maintain the body's status quo. The reduction in their activity occurs so slowly that the changes that result are not immediately perceptible. It is only by looking back at functions we once took as natural, when we were young, that we come to realise that there has been a reduction in their efficiency.

These changes come to affect not only the way we look but also the way we feel and think. This process is well illustrated by the slow but inevitable reduction in the body's sexual functions. As the secretion of sex hormones begins during adolescence, the so-called 'secondary' sexual features develop. In the boy the penis enlarges, pubic hair begins to grow, typically peaking in the midline from the pubis to the bellybutton, or navel. The voice deepens as the larynx enlarges and facial hair appears.

With these physical changes come the emotional changes of puberty and the occurrence of penile erection. Similar changes occur in girls, resulting in vaginal secretions, the development of the breasts, the typical female distribution of pubic hair and the start of the monthly periods. As in boys, the hormones also have a profound effect on behaviour. Their effects are both physical and mental.

As we get older we come to regard our sexual activity as a badge of adulthood with a peak in its activity at around twenty to thirty years. In fact, hormonal activity peaks considerably earlier and is actually well past its prime by the age of thirty. We compensate for this by developing the subtleties of lovemaking and substitute sophistication as a replacement for the small but measurable loss of hormonal activity.

At birth, we have a complete lifetime's stock of ova and sperm cells. It is believed that few if any more ova are produced as a result of hormonal activity. It is this bank of life that we call upon during procreation. Fortunately, the ova do not age significantly so long as they are maintained in a suitable environment. Unlike other cells in the body, the nucleus with its content of chromosomes, does not suffer the ravages of reduction by free radicals found in the rest of the cells in the body. Nevertheless, there is good statistical evidence that the ova of older mothers do produce a higher number of children with birth defects such as Down's syndrome and cleft palate. It is as though the best eggs get broken most easily and are lost to the reproductive process leaving a legacy of more robust but less perfect cells. It is generally advised that mothers-to-be who are over the age of 35–40 should be screened and the foetus tested (a procedure called *amniocentesis*) to detect potential serious birth defects.

By the time we come to retire, most of us will be less concerned with sexual activity as a prelude to procreation, but rather as a means of satisfying our physical, psychological and emotional feelings. In spite of this, men continue to release sperm during sexual activity long after the female has reached the menopause and stopped releasing ova. There are many cases of men with young partners who have fathered children while in their late seventies; however, there is a significantly greater risk of foetal abnormalities associated with late fatherhood.

To most men planning their retirement, the prospect of fathering a young child would cause consternation at the thought of this late, additional responsibility. Nevertheless, it appears that some women continue to feel a sense of emptiness and loss following the menopause and it is not uncommon for them to seek a chance to foster or adopt a child and, in rare, highly publicised cases, to have a baby by *in vitro* implantation (artificial insemination).

In some religious sects, the emotional aspect of sex is ignored and sexual activity is firmly tied to procreation, as it is in most of the animal kingdom. As a result, sexual intercourse after childbearing takes on the nature of a sin. This rule seems to have been applied more resolutely to women than to men! However, it was not uncommon in past times for women to regard sexual intercourse as a duty, which ceased at the menopause.

The concept of sex as a pleasurable and enjoyable act is largely a result of the introduction of safe, cheap contraception and the subsequent separation of sexual intercourse simply as a prelude to child bearing from it as a physiological and emotional activity. It was once taken for granted that women would not welcome sex once they had reached the menopause and could no longer bear children. I still find it difficult to imagine that my grandparents would ever have indulged in sexual intercourse because, when I was a youth, they always appeared to be old and sex was associated with being young. Such has been the sexual revolution, that today's youth assume a sexual activity in their grandparents that is often flattering but beyond their physical capabilities.

The menopause

The menopause occurs when the diminution in the production of female sex hormones reaches a critical level. It occurs in women in their forties to early fifties, although the exact time of its occurrence is unpredictable. Generally, if the woman's periods had started at an early age, the menopause will tend to be later than it would in someone whose periods did not commence until age thirteen or fourteen.

There is little doubt that the endocrine turmoil that occurs at the time of the menopause has a profound effect upon the physiological balance of various systems in the body, while the psychological effect of this milestone in a woman's life varies greatly from person to person with less predictable consequences. The result of the sharp reduction in the cycle of hormonal influences, that of oestrogen followed by progesterone, affects other endocrine systems and increases the sensitivity of many processes in the body to the effects of chemical transmitters such as adrenalin and serotonin. This produces sudden, unprovoked effects upon the cardio-vascular system, the temperature-controlling mechanisms, appetite and the emotions.

Only a women who has experienced the sudden heat that seems to develop from within the body, leading to flushing and sweating, can appreciate its discomfort. The palpitations and blood-pressure fluctuations that occur may cause anxiety and headaches and often result in the mistaken diagnosis of a heart attack. Indeed, in the ten years following the menopause, women are most vulnerable to heart attacks and strokes. The emotional changes can cause a rational, stoical woman to burst suddenly into tears or to magnify what she saw as a minor problem previously into an insuperable obstacle.

Insomnia is commonplace at this time. Some fortunate women, usually those with a late menopause, find these symptoms merely annoying, but to those more seriously affected they are an affliction. Although the symptoms are self-limiting, usually becoming less and less severe over about one to two years, it is understandable that many women seek to mitigate their effect by hormone replacement therapy.

Hormone-replacement therapy

HRT was originally introduced to allay the most severe menopausal symptoms and as a prophylactic treatment to prevent osteoporosis, which afflicts so many women following the menopause. It was found to provide other benefits, such as a feeling of wellbeing, and to delay the onset of sexual and physical ageing. As a result, treatment is often prolonged or, especially in America, started during the postmenopausal years as a remedy for ageing. In recent times, large studies have revealed that some forms of treatment in certain groups of women increase the risks of cancer of the breast and of strokes. This effect is quite small and is less likely to occur with treatment tailored to the needs of each individual.

Nevertheless, the general advice – to start treatment just before the menopause and to use it for about five years – is sensible. If it is continued for a longer period it is associated with an increased breast-cancer risk of about 1–2 per cent over a ten-year period. Women with a bad family history of breast or ovarian cancer should avoid HRT, as should those with high blood pressure.

Male menopause

Although this is a subject promoted in pop psychology, there is no true equivalent of the menopause in men. The slow rundown in the production of male hormones is not associated with any sudden physiological or emotional changes; as a result, the desire and ability for sexual intercourse continues unabated, if at a slightly reduced level.

Sex in later life

There is a subtle emotional change associated with sexual activity as we get older. In the young, sexual activity is associated with an urgent, aggressive attitude reminiscent of many animals' courtship. In later life, it is a more sophisticated pleasure rather than the relief of a passionate urge. Like a good wine, it is to be savoured rather than slurped. The frequency of such activity invariably diminishes with age.

For the female, dryness of the vagina (in the absence of HRT) and erectile problems in the male may impair the satisfaction of sexual intercourse. The inability to obtain a satisfactory erection is a common problem in men as they get older. Without the necessary tumescence, sensation from the penis is greatly reduced, making ejaculation difficult. The availability of drugs such as Viagra has helped to overcome this problem.[1] The effect of these drugs on the

1 Although Viagra was the first commercially available drug to treat erectile dysfunction, its effect has a very short duration. Longer-acting drugs are now available that many find more satisfactory. Your GP will advise you of the most appropriate treatment.

penis (its *vasculature*) was discovered by accident when their use was being investigated for the treatment of heart failure due to constriction of the blood vessels in the lung! (Viagra is still used to combat heart failure due to a sudden ascent to a high altitude.) Before they became available, it was fashionable, in some circles, to use amyl nitrate, a pill prescribed for the relief of angina. It probably worked in much the same way as Viagra but was often associated with a precipitous, dangerous fall in blood pressure. Drugs such as Viagra should be used with caution, as they may cause the blood pressure to fall, migraine headaches and a painful, irreducible erection of the penis if given in an overdose.

One word of caution, sexual intercourse is often the most extreme form of exercise that many older people encounter and it is not uncommon for it to provoke angina; in a few cases it may cause a heart attack. It is sensible to avoid such a stress immediately after a heavy meal.

'Nip down to Boots again will you...I need a top up.'

Chapter Nine
Taking a Health Check

As we get older it is natural to become more concerned about our health. Regular health checks are strongly recommended in order to prevent a minor problem from turning into a major disease. There's an assumption that if a disease is spotted early it can be nipped in the bud and widespread damage prevented. This approach is reasonable and is indeed valid for many diseases; unfortunately, there are some medical problems that occur as we get older that cannot be easily resolved, however early they are diagnosed.

Many of the symptoms complained about by the over-sixties, such as muscular aches, joint and back pains, tiredness, loss of memory, breathlessness and a 'lack of go', are not necessarily caused by a pathological or a reversible process. Nevertheless, it is these complaints that cause the over-sixties to form such a large proportion of the patients swamping doctors' surgeries.

In previous chapters, we've looked at the various bodily changes that take place as we get older. The rate and the intensity with which these effects develop varies greatly from person to person. This is often due to genetic factors, as demonstrated by studies on identical twins brought up in different environments who usually develop the same 'wear-and-tear diseases' at about the same age. However, the stresses and strains of life and the type of lifestyle and diet pursued also play a part in the development of symptoms associated with these changes.

When you retire, it is sensible to check on the significance of any symptoms that may develop, while accepting that some changes are due to the ageing process and are an inevitable part of living longer. It is because some of these symptoms may be the harbinger of future medical problems, which, if treated early may prevent a later medical catastrophe, that regular checkups are advised.

In the young, nonspecific medical checkups generally have a high-cost–low-benefit ratio, but this is greatly reduced as we get older. Medical checkups are to be encouraged in anyone over fifty. Specific checkups for a particular genetic susceptibility – such as colonoscopy for those with a family history of bowel cancer and ultrasound screening of the ovaries in those with a family history of breast and ovarian cancer – are cost-effective in all age groups

Some so-called checkups are so cursory as to be useless. Indeed, by imbuing a sense of security, they may lead the patient into ignoring important early-warning signs and symptoms.

A checkup should start with a family history. Because a number of diseases are genetically determined, those that afflicted the parents are likely to be reproduced in their children. This is important in such conditions as cancer of the bowel, cancer of the breast and ovaries, high blood pressure and strokes, heart attacks and type 1 diabetes. There are many other diseases, such as diabetes type 2, in which it is probable that there is a genetic link, but, as it tends to occur in an older age group, it is more difficult to demonstrate such an association with certainty.

A detailed account of any present symptoms should be made and special attention paid to any unusual changes in bowel rhythm and the frequency of urination. Breathlessness and chest pain require more detailed questioning in order to determine if it is due to poor muscle tone and lack of physical fitness, or to heart and lung disease.

A physical examination should pick up incipient obesity, poor lung or cardiac function, any enlargement or displacement of the heart, irregularities in the heart's rhythm and the general condition of the body musculature. In women, the breast should be examined (physical examination is more likely to detect a rapidly growing, invasive cancer than mammography or X-ray screening). According to the nature of the symptoms described in the patient's history, specific tests such as a rectal examination, MRI scan or blood and urine checks may be indicated.

Specific tests should be carried out to assess blood fats and cholesterol, liver and kidney function, the presence of diabetes and gout (if appropriate). The haemoglobin and blood studies may indicate slow or hard-to-detect internal bleeding, such as that caused by a bowel polyp or a uterine fibroid.

Routine screening

Although breast screening in women is doubtfully cost-effective it is a source of reassurance and comfort to women over fifty, especially those with a history of breast lumps or those with a mother or sibling who suffered from cancer of the breast or ovary. The downside of this investigation is that it does not pick up all cancers and that many suspicious lumps turn out to be benign. This is because breast screening detects calcification and excessively hard scar tissue, and it is not specific for cancer. Indeed, the very cancers that are associated with calcification are those that grow very slowly and are therefore likely to be among the least aggressive types of tumour. Subjecting a women to a breast biopsy means that she suffers needless anxiety and undergoes an unnecessary surgical procedure.

Cervical smears have reduced the incidence of cancer of the neck of the womb significantly, despite the fact that the procedure detects many more lesions, as potential cancers, than were ever likely to have developed into actual invasive tumours.

The place of screening for prostate cancer in men using the PSA (prostate-specific antigen) test is more controversial. A raised PSA on its own is not evidence of prostate cancer. If an abnormal result is found, it is sensible to repeat the test at monthly intervals, and, if it does not return to normal, to carry out a prostatic biopsy.

There are many clinics that claim to be able to detect disease from examination of the patient's eyes or stool specimen. Their claims are without any scientific basis. Certainly, examination of the back of the eye by an expert with an ophthalmoscope can detect signs of diabetes and high blood pressure, as well as eye disease, but it tells us little about other diseases.

There are certain rare digestive disorders that cause changes in the composition of faeces, but generally the composition of the stools varies little unless the diet is altered, although they may be affected by any bowel infection. They tell you nothing about general health and are useless as a means of diagnosing anything, except intestinal infections and bleeding.

Claims have been made that examination of the blood by mysterious, complex instruments allows a diagnosis of some specific food allergies that are the cause of general ill health. These claims should be treated with scepticism.

Early diagnosis

Early diagnosis may prevent a curable disease from becoming incurable or of causing secondary effects in other organs. However, these situations are less frequent than is commonly believed.

That said, the early treatment of high blood pressure may prevent irreversible changes in the heart and cardiovascular system. And type 2 diabetes can occur insidiously and, if it is left untreated, can affect eyesight and the kidney function.

Anyone with a family history of cancer of the bowel should have regular colonoscopies performed. This cancer almost always starts as a small polyp causing few if any symptoms. At this stage it is curable, but, if left until it is sufficiently large to obstruct the bowel, it is likely to have spread to other parts of the body and be incurable.

Patients with several family members who have suffered from breast or ovarian cancer may possess an *oncogene* (a cancer-causing gene) that renders them particularly susceptible to these diseases. They should be kept under close supervision and precautionary surgery may be indicated.

Unfortunately, there are many diseases and some cancers where symptoms appear only once the disease is well advanced, and there are some where an early diagnosis does not make the condition any easier to treat. However, the general principle that the earlier the diagnosis is confirmed and treatment started the better the outcome holds true for most pathological processes and makes medical screening worthwhile, especially as we get older. There is little doubt that these checkups have contributed significantly to the increase in life expectancy that has occurred in all developed countries.

'Do you think we should downsize?'

Chapter Ten

Small is Beautiful: Downsizing

One of the pressing decisions on retirement is whether to stay in the same accommodation or to downsize. The decision is often complicated by:

- financial considerations caused by the loss of a regular income
- the onset of arthritis or heart problems that suggest that downsizing will soon become a matter of necessity
- the desire to find somewhere 'easier to run'

There is no doubt that being able to move to a home that is cheaper to purchase and to run releases capital tied up in bricks and mortar, reduces the weekly overheads and may provide a degree of financial flexibility. It usually makes better financial sense than indulging in a scheme for equity release in the present home, although both alternatives should be considered and advice sought from an independent expert.

The advantages of moving to a smaller home that has a smaller garden and that is easier to look after and maintain are not only financial: there can also be a psychological stimulus as you contemplate starting a new chapter in your life in a new environment – a chance to throw off the physical encumbrances of the 'old life'. There is little point in paying the overhead expenses of bedrooms that are not used and heating spaces that are kept empty. It may be the first twinges of arthritis or a bad family history of heart disease that makes it expedient to move to a home with fewer stairs and with less garden to maintain.

However, the decision to move should not be taken lightly. Downsizing means reducing your investment in property. If you trace the historical performance of such an investment in the last twenty years, it can be seen to have outperformed most other financial indices and the capital gain is tax-exempt. If there is no financial pressure to move, a case can certainly be made for maintaining your investment in your own house, as long as it is expedient.

There's good sense in postponing such a move until the right time. Moving home incurs considerable expense and upheaval. This may be another reason for not moving too soon unless you're absolutely certain that it will be a long-term solution. Too often, people move as soon as they retire, only to find that the new accommodation is too small for the grandchildren to stay overnight, the kitchen lacks eating space or one of them misses his or her study or workshop space.

Where to move

It is very common to find one of the pressing reasons given for moving is 'to be near the children'. This is a very understandable sentiment but it should be only one of the considerations that help shape a decision to downsize. Too often after moving to be near the children, a job opportunity takes them to another part of the country. Too close a proximity to a child may produce a hitherto unexposed friction in the relationship with his or her partner.

Although it's good to be able to see more of your grandchildren as they grow up, no grandparent is a substitute for your grandchildren's friends. Sooner or later, they will regard coming to see you as a duty and will eventually go off to be with their peers.

It's much more important and sensible to move to be

close to your friends. It is the ability to maintain friendships that should be the determining factor of life in retirement. To move away from friends isolates you from the very influences that keep you young and active. It is the constant discussions, the outings and the holidays with your peers that prevent you from becoming increasingly parochial once you've retired and no longer have the companionship provided by colleagues at work.

It is believed that it's through argument and conversation that we delay and reduce the inevitable memory loss. It helps to keep the recall of places and names accessible in our memory. It is friends who provide the encouragement necessary when adversity occurs and who will help you to celebrate any enjoyable occasion. Retirement is a time to cultivate and nurture friendships; any move that *threatens* the bonds of friendship are to be avoided.

In many instances it is the unfortunate or untimely death of a partner that leads to downsizing of accommodation. The ideal situation, in past times, was that of the Lord of the Manor upon whose death the wife would move to the dowager cottage in the grounds, leaving the manor to the next of kin. In this way she would maintain her status while living in more suitable accommodation.

There is much to be said for making a change at such a time. The necessary activity that surrounds such a move provides an antidote to the inevitable depression caused by the loss of one's partner. It disposes of memories of past shared events that are often painful to recall and it marks the start of a different lifestyle.

Everyone will have to decide for themselves whether or not to move and what will actually influence the decision as to when they move and to where. In all events it is not a decision to be made impulsively and without due consideration of all the possible consequences involved.

Too often, a hasty decision to 'move into the countryside' is influenced by a sunny weekend strolling along leafy lanes and lunches taken at thatched and oak-beamed country pubs. The truth of rural life becomes apparent only after moving, when the constant rain makes walking impossible, when your friends put off visiting in the dark days of winter and the villagers in the pub resent the stranger who has come into their midst. The move away from a town into the countryside can work, but it requires forward planning. It is sensible to try to rent a property in the area for a few months before making an irrevocable decision. Although this adds to the expense of downsizing, it might prevent you from making a very expensive mistake.

Supplementing income

One of the most popular ways of ensuring an extra income once you retire is to buy a property with the idea of supplementing your income from renting it out. Because of the considerable rise in the value of these investments over the past twenty years, it has delivered both an increasingly valuable asset and a steadily increasing income. The problem with this sort of investment is that, without the rise in property values, it can prove disastrous. It gambles on a rise in house prices continuing indefinitely. Because the actual realistic return on property investment is only about 3–4 per cent, allowing for fallow times between lets and for the cost of repairs, it requires a 3–4 per cent annual increase in house values to break even and produce the same return as the cost of a mortgage.

An alternative way to supplement income is from realising some of the value locked up in the house in which you live – so-called equity release. In its simplest form, it is taking out a mortgage for part of the value of your house and using the money provided to buy an investment that produces a higher return, after paying tax, than the mortgage. This is usually provided by an annuity, which will continue to produce income as long as you or your spouse is alive. Since an annuity is based on your life expectancy, this type of supplementary income becomes more attractive as you get older, especially if you have an illness that impairs your life expectancy. The disadvantage of this type of investment is that it reduces the capital value of your estate and so leaves less money to be passed on to any children.

It is important to determine your attitude to the possibility of passing on the residue of your estate to any children when considering ways of supplementing your retirement income. For anyone with a significant estate it should be borne in mind that when you and your spouse have died, 40 per cent of the estate (in excess of the nil-rate band) will pass to the Exchequer. For every £10,000 the government will take £4,000 in tax. By giving away the £6,000 to the children, in annual tax-free amounts, while you are alive, you ensure that they will receive the same inheritance, free of any tax, provided you live for a further seven years. You will then be left with the £4,000 extra to spend that would otherwise be paid in inheritance tax.

'It's just a passing phase officer !'

Chapter Eleven

A New Lifestyle?

You'll fill in the details of your lifestyle for yourself once you've retired from full-time work. The most that can be suggested is a template on to which you can graft your particular style of living. It is essential at the outset to confront certain inevitabilities, associated with the third age, that will set the parameters of any future endeavours. The first of these is that there is no *fourth* age. Missed opportunities are bound to be regretted and wasted chances are unlikely to come round again. It is a time to make use of every opportunity to enjoy your life.

In spite of the obvious fact that we should seize every opportunity to live as full and exciting a life as possible once we retire, financial considerations often come to assume a controlling influence on our choice of lifestyle. Since it's difficult to make good any serious loss of capital, the temptation is always to live within our income; this, together with the desire to be able to 'leave something for the children', often comes to restrict unreasonably the way we live.

The other important consideration in the third age is of living a healthy lifestyle and minimising any risk to health, even if this means avoiding a new experience.

It's obviously important to plan your expenses with a degree of caution, but too often excessive prudence results in a failure to seize a unique opportunity to go somewhere or do something expensive or exotic and leads to years of regret later. This is especially true when it comes to group activities: a failure to share the experiences of your friends may result in regrets that cannot easily be forgotten.

Planning your lifestyle

It is because the working week lasted from Monday to Friday that the weekends assume such importance in our lives. Without a weekly break, one day becomes exactly like another, and the sense of expectation, produced as the week advances towards the weekend, is lost. Retirement gives us the freedom to choose when to have the break that punctuates the week. Many of us will continue to do this at the weekend, because it fits in with family activities, but there is much to be said for starting the 'weekend' on Friday morning so as to avoid the crowds that are restricted by the pattern of their work. It also means we can extend the break to Monday if the occasion permits.

These weekly breaks should be varied and planned in advance, whenever possible. To do the same thing every weekend is dull and a recipe for boredom. The weekend becomes a chore, not a pleasure. However, not to plan in advance will result in frustration and recrimination. The break may centre on a visit to the theatre, a dinner with friends or having the grandchildren to stay. At least some of these breaks should be away from the home environment.

If feasible, one weekend in six should be spent doing something very different, such as staying in the country and going for walks, visiting relatives in a different part of the country or going on a weekend break to a foreign city. Many affinity groups organise these types of break. Gardening clubs visit rural gardens, angling clubs have away fishing weekends, art groups arrange visits to exhibitions and institutions arrange study weekends. These breaks are not only a pleasure in themselves, but also encourage an interest in what's going on around us, help us to make friends and to stimulate the mind. This is particularly true once one develops a particular knowledge or expertise in a subject – it can easily become a consuming and rewarding passion.

In addition to the weekend breaks, longer holidays should be planned to give as much variety and interest as possible. It is sensible to take one's longest holiday in January or February, when the short dark days are depressing, the cost of heating the home is highest and in many holiday resorts the cost of accommodation is low.

If you can afford to go south of the equator, you get the extra benefit of longer hours of daylight. There's good evidence that sunshine dispels depression through the secretion of endorphins, nature's happy hormone. Many retired people choose to holiday on a cruise. It's an ideal way to combine seeing new and exotic places in some luxury, while having the opportunity to enjoy the company of new acquaintances. Most cruises provide a good variety of entertainment and some arrange lectures by experts on places visited and other topics. A few cruises design their itinerary and entertainment especially for the over-fifties.

Activity holidays designed for the over-fifties are less common. Nevertheless, certain types of holiday do attract this clientele. Safari holidays are popular and offer a great way of enjoying seeing wild animals in natural surroundings. As they are gregarious holidays, involving travelling as a small group, they give an opportunity to have companionship during the day and friendship in the post-safari get-together around a campfire. City-centre visits are more likely to attract retired people than beach holidays, and tours of distant countries such as India and China are invariably heavily weighted with travellers who are over fifty.

For those who cannot afford these more exotic holidays, there are opportunities to rent self-catering accommodation in places such as the Costa del Sol, Portugal and Greece, where the weather is more benign than in the UK and life is a lot cheaper. Out-of-season apartments can often be rented at a fraction of the cost of a summer holiday. In order to enjoy this type of holiday it is best to go with friends, so that you have companionship during the occasional rainy day.

Having mapped out an approach to life in the third age that is sufficiently flexible to allow for unforeseen contingencies and personal preferences, it is necessary to develop a daily routine that is both stimulating and rewarding. Too many of those facing retirement dread the thought that on waking in the morning they can't find a good reason to get out of bed and start the day.

The fear of boredom is a recurring theme among retirees questioned at retirement seminars. It is noticeably more common among men than women. This fear often drives a man who has recently retired into making unreasonable and ill-considered demands on his wife or partner. Women frequently complain that they fear that spending all day, every day, with their menfolk will place an intolerable strain on their marriage. Too often they feel that they have bowed to the demands of a man who was at home only for the weekend and at work during the rest of the week because it was his only time with the family. But now, to be expected to comply with his wishes seven days a week becomes intolerable. The adage 'I married you for better or worse, not for seven days a week' becomes a *cri de coeur*. The first principle underlying any decision about everyday living is that it must be acceptable to both parties.

An increasing number of men and women approaching retirement make arrangements to continue in part-time work or agree to be available at times of need in the workplace. This is an excellent arrangement in many cases, since it allows a period of adjustment to the altered circumstances and prevents an abrupt fracture of relationships and friendships with colleagues. It is always a temporary phase and should be regarded as a transitional period.

A more difficult situation arises when one partner is obliged to retire completely while the other is in full- or part-time employment. This usually affects men whose wives and partners are reaching the peak of their careers as they approach retirement. The work ethic and the routine are usually so strongly imbued in most of those who have worked for forty or so years that it is impossible for the man suddenly to adopt the role that most wives accept: that of a househusband. This situation should be anticipated and suitable arrangements made long before the problem becomes imminent.

Being aware of the likely problems that may occur when retirement finally arrives makes it easier to develop a suitable daily routine. Whatever is decided, it should allow plenty of time for spontaneous activities. It should be regarded as a framework, not as a straitjacket, and it should not impose a limitation on any pleasurable pursuit.

It might be appropriate to set aside one evening each week for a group activity such as bridge, a club activity or an evening class, and another for going to the theatre or cinema. Be cautious about making a set time or day for visiting relatives or children each week, as they might come to see any change in routine as a sleight.

It is sensible to get up in the morning at a set time. Lying in bed should be an occasional indulgence. The mornings may be spent in necessary household chores and attending to bills and services. Whenever possible, set aside one afternoon a week for an intellectually stimulating pursuit.

This could be a further-education class, a lecture, a book club, an Open University course or a self-teaching session. Keeping your mind active and embracing new ideas helps in preventing memory loss and makes you better able to adapt to the new way of life.

Many people study for higher diplomas once they retire. This is an excellent way of stretching the mind and improving your enjoyment of a hobby or pursuit. It's sensible to see these courses as a means to an end rather than as a challenge. It is likely that younger students with a more adaptable memory will outperform students in their sixties in any course of study that puts a premium on facts and figures. It is more sensible to study a subject that requires a breadth of knowledge or deductive ability.

Everyone will develop a particular lifestyle that will suit their own needs, but, within the week, time should be made available for regular exercise. A regular brisk daily walk with the dog may suffice if you have an active lifestyle but a two-to-three-mile walk three times a week is better. Attending regular exercise classes will help to keep you supple, and stretching exercises will help to prevent stiffening of joints, provided they are vigorous. Too often, these classes tend to cater for those who already have a physical restriction and are not sufficiently proactive to provide adequate exercise for a fitter person.

It is important to avoid a dull, repetitive lifestyle. Too many people spend every evening in front of a television screen after they retire, mindlessly watching whatever is provided. The programmes become a substitute for reading, discussion and independent thought. TV can set the parameters of your life – it is hopelessly restricting. The world becomes reduced to an existence limited by what this or that TV celebrity has dictated. Often meals come to play a subsidiary role, something to be fitted in to suit the TV schedule. The enjoyment of food is lost, as is good conversation. Life becomes constrained by takeaway meals and takeaway information. It is important to plan the evenings to bring a variety of interests as well as a mixed menu of foods.

It is imperative that those facing retirement realise the importance of friends in maintaining their outside interests. The place of friendships is central to building a sense of belonging and to developing an affinity group of 'people like us'. It may be necessary to initiate contacts or to follow up introductions in order to network with acquaintances and to draw them into your circle of friends. It is not a time to wait patiently for invitations that may not come. It is your friends who will often determine the nature of the life you will enjoy in the third age.

'Are your slippers left in the middle of the room pointing in that
unusual manner an aide-mémoire, or are you just a slovenly git?'

Chapter Twelve

A Healthy Life

The health-food industry has burgeoned in recent times into a multibillion-pound concern whose benefits, to those who are induced to buy their products, are impossible to measure objectively. The principal target for the sale of these products is the over-fifties, who buy 90 per cent of all their products. It is suggested that they will prevent ill health, disease and the effects of ageing. All the evidence suggests that, in the vast majority of instances, these claims are ill founded.

In spite of the blandishments of the health-food industry, there is absolutely no diet, health food or way of life that will ensure a life that is longer or more disease-free than those who ignored their promises, ate a good mixed diet of food they liked and spent their money enjoying themselves.

Every year thousands upon thousands of people pour money into the pockets of these twenty-first-century snake-oil salesmen in the expectation that this or that remedy will stop them growing old or becoming arthritic, or that they will somehow achieve longevity. There is scant scientifically valid evidence that these potions make any difference to health – indeed some are potentially poisonous.

It is a testament to the power of advertising and to the gullibility of those buying these medicines that some treatments, such as 'Chinese herbs', have a vast sale in this country, whereas in China they are used only by those who cannot afford Western medicine. If they were effective, then the life expectancy of the Chinese might be expected to approach that of Europe – it does not.

The use of celebrities to promote a diet or an alternative lifestyle is a questionable practice that should provoke anyone thinking of signing up to such a treatment to question their qualification to promote such a product. Similarly, when a celebrity chef promotes a particular diet, you should question the depth of their knowledge about the workings of the digestive system and the physiology of human nutrition. Some are promoting a belief system and presenting it as a proven fact. When a self-styled 'expert nutritionist' tells you to eat this or that foodstuff you should realise that most nutritionists are self-taught.

Those entering the third age are the principal targets for the sale of these 'health foods'. They are rightly seen as the group most concerned about their health and most willing to pay for treatments that might ward off the ravages of the ageing process. Their advertising is unashamedly aimed at the fears of older people. The remarkable thing is that it is those in this age group who themselves help to promote these unproven treatments, because they feel they have derived some benefit from the money they have spent. It is because of this belief that it is difficult to prevent people wasting their money, although most of those treatments that have been investigated have not been found to affect any known pathological or physiological process.

Nevertheless, many of those who take these dubious remedies claim that they do produce a relief of their symptoms, rather like those who used to pour millions of pounds into the pockets of the patent-medicine charlatans. This is due to an ill-understood process called the *placebo effect*.

Doctors have been aware of this effect for many years. It used to be commonplace for a general practitioner to prescribe a harmless tablet of 'pink aspirin', assuring the patient that it was very potent and on no circumstance was the dose of one tablet a day to be exceeded. Unfortunately, present-day medical ethics prevent doctors from using this form of deceptive medicine, leaving the door open to the healthcare practitioners. The powers of positive persuasion of the prescriber, coupled with the desire on the part of the patient to achieve a positive benefit from their expenditure, often produce an improvement in the patient's symptoms. It is usual for any treatment, given with sufficient persuasion, to achieve an initial positive response in 10–15 per cent of patients. A slightly higher success rate often follows if the treatment involves the patient in active cooperation or in some physical discomfort. For example, a good acupuncturist will often achieve some perceived benefit in 20 per cent of his or her patients. Generally, the benefit is not permanent and the symptoms recur in days or weeks.

Subsequent treatments tend to be progressively less and less effective. What is surprising is that the benefit perceived by the patient occurs in spite of no change in the underlying pathology.

The other factor that complicates our understanding of the placebo response is that many medical conditions have periods when the symptoms are extreme and others when they are in remission and the patient appears to have recovered. It is too easy to ascribe any temporary improvement in the patient's condition to a particular herbal remedy or treatment rather than to the natural course of the disease.

Food additives and supplements

While a wide section of the population buy food supplements such as vitamins, garlic tablets, antioxidants and trace elements such as selenium and zinc, they are bought most extensively by the over-fifties in the belief that their body needs them. Health magazines suggest that, as we get older, we become more susceptible to vitamin and trace-element deficiencies. There is little scientific evidence that this is true provided we eat a normal diet. Indeed, there's scant evidence that they do anything to improve one's health. It is highly unlikely that anyone eating a varied mixed diet will suffer from a lack of these essential chemicals. Only those on an unusual or restricted diet, such as vegans or the anorexic, may require regular supplements.

Selenium, a common health-food additive, is present in the soil and is taken up by the vegetation and concentrated in seeds and nuts. It is present in a slightly higher concentration in wheat grown in the USA than in that grown in Europe. Plants grown artificially or in soil that is repeatedly flooded so that its minerals are washed away, as in rainforests, may lack selenium. Only very small amounts of selenium are required by the body – indeed, it is toxic in larger quantities.

In some societies it is usual not to expose the body, other than the face, to sunshine. With the prevalent scare stories about the dangers of sunshine, the levels of vitamin D in some Europeans (usually women) are lower than optimal. Without sunshine we may fail to produce sufficient vitamin D in our body and rickets may result.

Sunshine

In recent years the idea has been promulgated that sunshine is dangerous. Nothing could be further from the truth. Sunshine is essential for the formation of vitamin D in the body; it causes a feeling of wellbeing by releasing endorphin, nature's happy pill, into the circulation; it assists the normal sleep pattern by inhibiting the production of melatonin; and it causes the suntan that is nature's sun blocker, acting to prevent sunburn. Although it may cause a weather-beaten look to the skin, it is not the cause of wrinkles in the older person – indeed, it may reduce their number by causing a reaction similar to the anti-wrinkle creams.

There is no doubt that prolonged exposure to

ultraviolet light can cause skin cancer. These are basal cell carcinomas and epitheliomas, but they are very slow-growing and, except in very rare cases, do not metastasise – spread – to other parts of the body. They can easily be completely removed.

The scares about the malevolent effect of sunshine come from the fear that it may cause the dangerous skin lesion of malignant melanoma. There are those who feel so convinced of this association that they have led a crusade against sunshine. There is no convincing proof that malignant melanoma is caused by sunshine. If it were, it would be expected to be more prevalent on the exposed parts of the body, such as the hands and face. It is not. It occurs equally on most parts of the body, including the fingernails and soles of the feet. It also occurs around the anus! If it was caused by sunshine, one would expect it to be more prevalent in older people, like other skin cancers – it is not. It occurs equally frequently at all ages over puberty.

Whilst sun burn should be avoided, the dangers of sunshine are greatly exaggerated.

Vitamin C is an antioxidant and has been recommended, in huge doses, as a cure for the common cold. The evidence for such an action is unconvincing. We have a limited capacity to store this vitamin in the body and any excess rapidly passes into the urine. As with assertions as to the value of other antioxidants, the evidence that they do any good is largely anecdotal or it comes from epidemiological studies whose results are open to alternative interpretation.

A good example of this was the finding that the natives of Okinawa island eat large quantities of yams and that they lived longer than natives of neighbouring islands. This effect was attributed to the high antioxidant content of yams. In fact, it is probably due to the fact that the natives are ethnic Japanese, who also live longer when they do not consume yams.

Those few scientifically controlled studies that have been carried out fail to demonstrate any advantage to be gained in eating large quantities of antioxidants as fruit or vegetables (these studies are technically difficult, since it is almost impossible not to eat food that doesn't contain antioxidants).

There is a common assumption among those spending their money on vitamins and supplements that if a little of something is good for you a lot must be even better. While most of these chemicals have a low toxicity, the doses advocated by some so-called experts are worrying. Animal studies suggest that vitamins E and A may cause tissue damage in large doses. Vitamin B_6 is present in some vitamin supplements in amounts that, in animals, will cause nerve damage. Large doses of vitamin D have been implicated as a possible cause of kidney stones.

There has been recent interest in supplements of omega-3 fatty acids. Indeed, it has been added to some fatty products, which are then labelled as 'extra-healthy'. These fats form part of the coating of the cells of our body and are especially important in the cells of the brain. There is some evidence of a benefit from a high intake in dyslexic children. A review of some forty trials using these supplements has failed to reveal any short-term benefits in adults.

Herbal remedies

Many present-day drugs have been developed from herbal remedies. Examples of such chemicals are digitalis, quinine, penicillin and morphine. There is no doubt that some herbal remedies do contain chemicals that are active in the body and may be useful in the treatment of diseases. The pharmaceutical industry has spent many millions of pounds trying to isolate these substances, sometimes, as with penicillin, with remarkable consequences for medicine.

Unfortunately, plant chemicals are unpredictable. The mixture of substances extracted from a plant may include some that are toxic. The proportion of active to toxic ingredients may vary according to the method of abstraction, the time of year when it is harvested, the climatic conditions in which it was grown and the part of the plant, flower, leaf or seed used to prepare the medicine. The content of active drug is never controlled and any ill effects of the medication go unrecorded. As a result, while there may well be some herbal remedies that may help treat certain diseases that remain undiscovered, the risks associated with the use of some plant remedies are considerable. Poisoning by these medicines is common.

Alternative treatments

Scientific studies of osteopathy have demonstrated it to be useful in the treatment of musculoskeletal problems, especially those associated with back strain. Its success rate, carried out by competent trained practitioners, is equal to, or in some cases better than, conventional medical treatment. All other forms of alternative treatment such as acupuncture, homeopathy, reflexology and Ayurvedic medicine fail to achieve results much better than those of any placebo in scientifically valid trials. Their success rate depends on the skill of practitioners in 'selling' themselves and the treatment, and desire of the patient to obtain a good result.

These alternative therapies flourish in those conditions commonly labelled as *psychosomatic* (i.e. the mind's effect on the body), which are not amenable to conventional medicine. What is important is not to end up being treated for a curable medical condition by an alternative therapist who may aggravate an underlying problem or delay effective treatment. It is vital to establish a diagnosis and to find out if conventional medicine can offer a treatment before embarking on any alternative therapy. Always try to assess whether the alternative treatment is doing any good by means of objective tests such as bending and straight-leg raising after treatment for back pain, ability to sleep at night without painkillers and so on.

If conventional medicine held all the answers and could offer effective treatments for all our ailments, alternative medicine and herbal 'cures' would disappear. That they flourish is an indication of the shortcomings of present-day medical practice. Before embarking on an expensive course of alternative treatment, we should pause to reflect that, if we really *did* know of a herb or an unconventional treatment that actually *did* cure a disease, it would have been taken up by doctors and the pharmaceutical industry and used as part of normal medical practice.

'Well you have the heart of an ox...unfortunately though, one that's overweight, overworked and over the hill.'

Chapter Thirteen

Weighty Matters

Middle-age spread and obesity are common problems as one approaches the third age. Although obesity undoubtedly contributes to ill health as one gets older, it is almost inevitable that as height decreases there will be a thickening of the trunk and the development of some degree of potbelly. No amount of dieting or exercise will change this, and there is no evidence that it does us any harm.

The media would have us believe that to be overweight is likely to lead to a rapid demise; this is not true. Only if the obesity is truly gross, in excess of 20 per cent greater than the accepted body-mass index, or BMI, does it interfere with the enjoyment of a normal life span, although it may limit enjoyment of a particular lifestyle. (See the box in Chapter 5 for how to calculate your BMI.) It is sensible to control any increase in weight as we get older by adjusting the way we live rather than by opting for a restricted diet or a rigorous regime of exercise.

The actual way we measure obesity tends to discriminate against older people, especially those who have lost height. The measurement of height is squared to form the denominator in determining the BMI and as a result any reduction becomes exaggerated. As we saw in Chapter 5, before 2000, most statistics were based on the Metropolitan Life Assurance figures, and to compare the incidence of obesity measured by this means with those obtained using the BMI is to compare apples with oranges – it is meaningless. The very best assessment of obesity comes from standing in front of a mirror and viewing one's figure. Gross abdominal obesity, pendulous abdominal fat and an inability to see one's toes are definite warning signs that action is required to lose weight. The trouble is that the fatter one gets the more difficult it becomes to lose weight.

Why lose weight?

The idea that we are in the middle of an epidemic of obesity and that we are going to die younger than our parents is absolute nonsense. Although there are more fat people around, there is no epidemic. Obesity itself does not kill, although the incidence of domestic accidents is higher among truly fat people. Obesity in the over-fifties is associated with a increased risk of type 2 diabetes, although the disease also occurs in thin people. It is as if the insulin-producing cells in the pancreas become exhausted by having to deal with so much carbohydrate.

Type 2 diabetes predisposes to a deterioration in the eyesight, to a rise in blood cholesterol, to kidney disease and a predisposition to arterial disease and heart attacks. These effects are insidious and are largely preventable by keeping the blood sugar in check either by adopting a suitable diet or by means of medicines. Although statistically there may be a shorter life expectation in those suffering this disease, by and large, provided care is taken to control the blood sugar, the effects are minimal.

Probably of greater significance is the effect of carrying around so much extra body weight. This imposes a burden on the heart and is often associated with an increase in the blood pressure. Cardiac failure and breathlessness often follow. The joints and tendons suffer from the strain of supporting the extra load. Arthritis and backache are common. These, together with the strain on the heart, lead to an increasingly sedentary lifestyle and a further increase in weight.

There is no scientific reason why obesity should cause cancer – it almost certainly does not. However, the incidence of some cancers is said to be marginally higher in fat people.

Losing weight

The body balances the calories it takes in – from food that has been eaten and digested and absorbed into the bloodstream – with those it uses as energy. Any excess calories will be laid down as fat or stored as glycogen in the liver. The concept that body fat comes only from eating fat is wrong. It comes from eating more of any food than the body requires.

The source of the calories does not matter to the body, but the conversion of any extra protein to fat requires energy. This is called the *specific dynamic action* of protein and in general is why, gram for gram, protein is less fattening than fat and carbohydrate. Although each gram of fat is roughly twice as fattening as carbohydrate, carbohydrates tend to cause more water retention than fat. A low-carbohydrate diet causes the most rapid loss of weight due partly to loss of water that accompanies it. Carbohydrate taken as sugars or alcohol causes an insulin surge and tends to promote hunger. The magnitude of this effect is called the *glycaemic index* (GI index).

The body uses energy to maintain vital activities such as those involved in the contraction of the heart, the working of the brain, metabolism in the liver and excretion by the kidneys; but the greatest amount of energy is spent in maintaining the body temperature and in sweating, especially in hot weather. As much as 80 per cent of all the energy used by the body at rest is expended in warming the body. Even in hot weather, the amount hardly decreases. The body is relatively inefficient as a machine: it wastes a lot of the energy in the form of heat. It compares badly with a modern motor car! Like a car, it utilises carbon-based fuel, in the form of sugars, to drive it and produces carbon dioxide in the process. In vigorous exercise it becomes even more inefficient, using only a small part of the calories locked into sugar to produce energy, forming lactic acid as a by product.

Excess heat production adds to its inefficiency, as energy has to be used to produce sweat in order to stop the body overheating. Because of the limitations on exercise as one gets older, it is not often a useful way of using up fat in order to lose weight. Regular exercise does, however, have some value, as it gears up body metabolism and this helps to reduce the amount of fat laid down. It follows that those whose body shape favours heat loss – that is, those who are tall and thin – use more energy maintaining body temperature than those who are more rotund. This is one of the reasons why fat people find it hard to lose weight.

Undoubtedly there are some people who seem to be able to eat as much as they like without putting on weight and others who find it difficult to lose weight while on a strict diet. There are differences in the way different people's bodies handle food and in their basal metabolism; however, these are exceptional.

There is only one reason we put on weight: it is because we take in more calories than our body uses. The only scientific way to lose weight is to reduce the amount we eat. The idea that this or that diet will cause us to lose weight and sustain a weight loss misses the essential point – to lose weight we must eat less. *What* we eat is less important than the *amount* we eat. This was shown by the initial success of the Atkins diet, which advocated a high-fat regime, although each gram of fat contains twice as many calories as carbohydrate or protein.

If there were an effective diet to lose weight, we would need only one. The fact that there are new diets every week is evidence that it is not what but how much you eat that counts. It is for this reason that researchers working in this field are concentrating on finding out what factors – including levels of leptin and insulin – control appetite.

In order to lose weight, all snack foods should be banned. Eating between meals, especially while watching television, is disastrous. Reducing alcohol intake to two to three units a day may help, but if the weight is not reducing then one meal a day should be omitted or taken in the form of a soup. Fruit should be eaten sparingly – soft fruit is fattening as is fruit juice. It is better to eat vegetables and salads if you feel deprived of antioxidants. In order to reduce the temptation to 'nibble' one should clear food away from the table once a meal has been finished. Housewives working in the kitchen, surrounded by food, need to adopt a strict discipline to prevent them from 'grazing' while cooking.

What is a unit of alcohol?

Nutritionists and health experts talk of 'units' of alcohol, and usually say one unit is equivalent to a half-pint of ordinary-strength beer, a 125 ml glass of wine or one measure of spirit. The equivalent metric measure is 10 millilitres or about 8 grams of ethanol, which is the active chemical in alcoholic drinks.

Some drinks are stronger than others, of course, and usually a measure called the ABV (alcohol by volume) is given on the bottle or bar pump. How do you tell whether that pint of real ale you've just ordered is, at 4 per cent ABV, equivalent to two units?

It can be determined by multiplying the volume of your drink in millilitres by its ABV and then dividing by 1,000. So a pint (or 568 millilitres) of beer at 4 per cent ABV would give you about 2.3 units. This is ascertained by multiplying 568 by 4 (the ABV), which gives you 2,272, and then dividing by 1,000, giving you 2.272, or, to round it up, 2.3. A pint of beer that is 5 per cent ABV would give you 2.84 units.

Drinking 3 units of alcohol a day is actuarially associated with a longer life expectancy than either drinking no alcohol or over 6 units a day.

You should aim for a slow but sustainable weight loss while eating as wide a variety of foods as you enjoy. Diets that prevent you from eating the sort of food you like are difficult to sustain and tend to be boring – after all, good food, good wine and good conversation are the cornerstones of a happy lifestyle.

'I'm afraid my wife's grown quite
intolerant to certain foods.'

Chapter Fourteen

Healthy Eating

In spite of what we read in the newspapers, see on television or hear on the radio, there are no such things as bad foods and good foods. Government agencies, under pressure from highly-motivated media-savvy pressure groups, some of which do not understand nutrition, have introduced a traffic-light system, ostensibly to allow the easily bamboozled shopper to distinguish between so-called 'healthy food' and 'unhealthy food'. The system is rightly being resisted by many food distributors as it condemns many important foods by labelling them as dangerous. Anchovies are condemned because of their high salt content but, leaving aside the issue of whether more people die from too little salt than too much, one uses anchovies very sparingly, as a garnish for pizzas, veal and so forth.

Many sauces earn red labels because they are high in oils and salt but the amount used is usually too small for this to be a problem. Hamburgers are given a red label if they contain fat, but a fat-free hamburger is tasteless and chewy – it needs an oily, sugary sauce such as ketchup to make it palatable. However, minced meat in lasagne and shepherd's pie is OK.

You cannot have fat-free yoghurts or cheese, and efforts to reduce the salt level of cheeses are futile, since they make age-old 'recipe cheeses' that have a unique and individual taste similar to all others.

The system of traffic-light labelling fails to understand the first truism of nutrition that Paracelsus (1493–1541), the Swiss alchemist, physician and astrologer, declared in the sixteenth century: every food and drink taken *beyond its dose* is a poison. It is not the food substance that is potentially hazardous: it is the *amount* you eat that decides whether or not it will do harm.

The second important principle it ignores is that there are no such things as 'good foods' and 'bad foods', although there are good and bad diets.

The media concept of 'junk food' is equally silly – the

term is an oxymoron. Either a food contains some nutrition, be it carbohydrate, protein or fat, in which case it is not junk, or it is devoid of nourishment, in which case it is not a food. The term is used by so-called nutritionists to deride cheaper cuts of meat, hamburgers, reconstituted meat and prepared foods. It ignores the biological fact that all meat, whether it be from an Angus fillet steak or from corned beef, is digested in the gut and absorbed into the bloodstream as the same amino-acid building blocks.

While reconstituted corned beef and Spam are now banned from school meals, the British Dietetic Association booklet on healthy eating for the older person recommends the use of corned-beef fritters because they are cheap and nutritious. Prepared foods are often the most convenient way for a single or an elderly person to obtain sufficient variety of foods in their diet.

Most of them are prepared under very tightly controlled, hygienic conditions and fulfil the one essential criterion for any food: they are enjoyed by those who eat them. This is far safer than food prepared locally in conditions that may encourage the growth of pathogenic bacteria. While a total diet of prepared foods would be expensive and unsatisfactory, they have a role to play in meeting the nutritional demands of the population. The idea that we would suddenly become a healthier nation if everyone prepared their own bolognese sauce for their spaghetti rather than buy that prepared on a large scale by experts is ludicrous.

It is understandable that celebrity chefs turn their noses up at the cheaper cuts of meat: they are usually more difficult to make into attractive meals and often do not carve easily into attractive slices. But at the end of the day they have a similar nutritional value to cheaper alternatives. What is required is wholesome, pathogen-free meat that makes a meal that can be enjoyed by those eating it. To be frightened off a product by the 'food police' because of a traffic-light label is silly.

A balanced diet

As we get older, food plays a more important role in our lives. Meals not only have a nutritional importance but they also come to play a part in cementing relationships and in promoting companionship. Although the pattern of three meals a day is often maintained, the evening meal usually plays a dominant role. It is imperative to make sure it is well balanced and nutritious. This means that it should contain carbohydrate, fat and protein. The form in which each component is taken doesn't matter, although if too much of the carbohydrate is taken in the form of sugar it is likely to cause an insulin surge and be less likely to satisfy the appetite – it should be avoided if you are trying to lose weight.

The best source of protein is in meat, but often our appetite for meat diminishes as we get older. Chicken, guinea fowl and fish are good alternative sources of protein. You shouldn't be unduly concerned about the fat content of the meat, since it invariably contributes greatly to the taste (if you've ever eaten an ostrich steak, you'll realise that lean meat is relatively tasteless). There is little difference, in terms of its nutritional effect, between the fat in meat and that in cheese. It is pointless to eat lean meat in the belief it is especially good for you and then to follow it with cheese. Because of the high rate of intestinal bacterial contamination in chickens, it is recommended that they should always be adequately cooked. Resistance to these bacteria is reduced as we get older.

Vegetarians need to seek alternative sources for their protein. There's a little protein in rice and in various seed vegetables, beans and eggs, but artificial sources of protein may be required to meet their needs. A vegetarian lifestyle is quite compatible with a normal life span without supplements but vegans need additional vitamin B_{12}, since this occurs only in the animal world.

Studies of the dental pattern of mankind, its digestive system and liver leave no doubt that, anthropologically and biologically, we are best suited to a mixed-meat-and-plant diet. We are not designed to be vegetarians.

In recent years it has become a widely held belief that we should eat less and less fat so as to reduce the blood cholesterol levels and the risk of heart attacks. This belief is ill conceived and wrong. Unless you eat an excessive amount of fat, it doesn't affect your coronary blood vessels or 'stuff your arteries with cholesterol'. It has been known for many years that a high dietary fat intake was not necessarily associated with a high incidence of heart disease, with the exception of some specific ethnic groups, such as those in Finland.

In one of the largest and longest-controlled studies (Rockefeller University, New York, 2006) it was found that there was no difference in the incidence of heart disease, heart attacks or cancer of the colon or breasts between those on a low-fat diet and those who eat as much fat and as many eggs as they liked. The anticipated association between saturated fats and heart disease was not demonstrated. This confirmed the findings of many other, less well-controlled investigations. It is known that the cholesterol in the atheromas in your arteries does not come from the cholesterol in the food you eat (we talked briefly of atheromas in Chapter 6). Cholesterol is made primarily in the liver, an effect depressed by statin drugs.

In the move away from butter in the 1970s and 1980s, there was an increased demand for margarine that was easy to use and cheap. This need was meet by increasing the amount of trans-fats in the product (trans-fats are unsaturated fats formed by hydrogenation in the manufacture of spreads). Much of this cheap margarine went into biscuit manufacturing. It is now suggested, as a result of animal experiments, that eating a lot of trans-fat may be carcinogenic.

We were told that we needed to eat a certain amount of roughage to keep our bowels regular and to prevent cancer of the colon. This is no longer believed. Astronauts on a very low-roughage diet still have their bowels open regularly, although at less frequent intervals, and roughage does not prevent cancer of the colon. Nevertheless, a certain amount of bulk gives one a comfortable, satiated feel after a meal and there is a little evidence that it may lower the incidence of heart disease.

Vitamins and trace minerals, especially iron, are required to meet the metabolic needs of the body. Fresh, lightly cooked green vegetables and meat products are a ready source of these essential elements of diet. Almost all normal diets provide an adequate supply of these chemicals. Meat, especially liver, is an excellent source of iron. Contrary to popular belief, spinach is not the best source of iron. Calcium requirements tend to be reduced as one gets older but it is sensible to ensure an adequate intake of calcium in the form of milk products, eggs and cheese, as a high intake plays a role in preventing osteoporosis.

It is recommended that we take in about 3 litres of water a day. To understand why, we need to consider the role of the kidney. The kidney possesses a large passive filter bed through which about 10–12 litres of water, containing salt, sugar and waste products, is filtered off each day. An efficient kidney then reabsorbs about 90 per cent of the water, virtually all the sugar and as much salt as it needs. Taking in more water does not wash out any extra waste products; it does not 'detoxify' the body as claimed by certain celebrities. It merely means less of the filtered water is reabsorbed and one runs to the toilet more frequently. Only if the kidneys are failing and losing their reabsorption capacity is it desirable to drink more water.

We take about 1.5–2 litres of water in a day in our food. All food contains water – some, such as vegetables and cucumbers, may be 95 per cent water. We need to drink about 1–2 litres a day as fluid. It doesn't matter if this is as beer, coffee, fruit juice or plain water. It is equivalent to about six cups of fluid a day.

As we get older, the enormous reserve capacity of the kidney becomes progressively reduced and a smaller proportion of the water filtered off is reabsorbed. We tend to urinate more frequently. As a result, it is often sensible to increase our fluid intake. This is especially true in hot weather or after exercise, as the body is also less efficient and we sweat more in order to lose heat. Remember, sweat contains a lot of salt and in these circumstances it is essential to increase our salt intake to prevent dehydration (see 'Salt' below).

One of the strangest campaigns in the present irrational frenzy of activity by the food police is the one against fizzy drinks. The fizz in these drinks is carbon dioxide, a substance we produce by the litre in our gut. Drinks such as Coca-Cola contain slightly fewer calories than a similar glass of orange juice.

Alcohol, tea and coffee

These drinks have recently had a bad press. There is no evidence that a modest intake of alcohol is bad for you or harmful to your health. Indeed, longevity statistics suggest that drinking up to three units per day increases your life span (see the box in Chapter 13, 'What is a unit of alcohol?'). Certainly, drinking more than six units will decrease your life expectancy. Epidemiological studies have failed to show any particular form of alcohol to be better than any other in this respect.

Tea and coffee have not been shown to cause any harmful effects in the body unless taken in excessive amounts. The ability of coffee to cause insomnia depends on dose. It takes very many cups of tea or coffee to increase the caffeine level in the blood to one that will cause insomnia. Your sleep is more likely to be disturbed by more trips to the toilet than by the effect of the caffeine.

Salt

There has been a recent campaign to reduce the amount of salt we eat in the belief that it is a major cause of high blood pressure. The rise in blood pressure with ageing is principally due to the changes that occur in the walls of the arteries and arterioles as we get older. Any dangerous increase in blood pressure can be effectively treated by drugs.

The part played by salt in high blood pressure is that of bit player cast as a villain. Taking in a large load of salt will cause a temporary increase in blood pressure until the body's mechanisms that maintain the fluid balance have dealt with it. There is little evidence that in the majority of people the level of salt intake has a permanent effect on the blood pressure. The Japanese eat about twice as much salt per day as we do in the UK. They do not suffer from more high blood pressure or strokes.

There is no convincing evidence that natives living in the Amazon Basin, where there is little salt in the soil, giving them a low-salt diet, live longer or healthier lives – indeed they add salt to their food whenever possible. Much of the experimental evidence is equivocal because different people respond differently to a salt load. There is no evidence that a low-salt diet reliably reduces blood pressure; indeed, in some studies it caused a rise in blood pressure in some people. High blood pressure should be treated with drugs; we know they work. A low-salt diet is miserable and in most cases it is ineffective.

The other side of this story is the danger of restricting salt. Healthy athletes die of heat stroke because of insufficient salt for them to sweat in order to lower their body temperature. Elderly people die in heat waves for the same reason. It is possible that a low-salt diet may lead to deep-vein thrombosis in those sitting still for over four hours. But the overriding consideration for taking in salt in our diet is that it adds taste to foods, especially watery ones such as soups. Those advocating a salt-free diet have lost sight of the purpose of eating, which is to take in sufficient nourishment to meet our metabolic needs. To this end we need to eat food that tastes good.

We should be cautious about accepting scare stories linking substances that have been present in food for many years to cancer in rats. Today we can detect the presence of chemicals at a level of one part per billion in food. Some of these chemicals can be shown to cause cancers when injected into or fed to rats. This does not necessarily imply they are harmful in humans in the doses we are likely to meet. Indeed, the chairman (from 2000 to 2005) of the Food Standards Agency, Professor Sir John Krebs, pointed out that one cup of coffee contains more substances that cause cancer in rats than that in the total food eaten in several months.

There has been a recent scare about acrylamide, a trace substance produced when food is barbecued or fried. Acrylamide does cause cancer in rats and has been present in our food since cavemen discovered fire and food was first cooked. There is a move to have its concentration in parts per million labelled in the contents of food. It is probable that a person would need to eat the equivalent of two barbecued cows to reach a level of acrylamide that would constitute a cancer risk.

Provided that we eat a mixed diet containing as great a variety of food as possible we do not need to worry about the latest scare from the food police. We should try to include some fresh ripe vegetables or fruit in our diet. If we are putting on weight we should eat less, possibly replacing one meal a day with a soup. There is no particular virtue in paying extra for expensive cuts of meat and no disadvantage in using prepared food as part of our diet.

As we age, the most important thing is to eat sufficiently and to enjoy what we eat.

'...Exactly how does this herbal remedy you've sold us
halt the ageing process?'

Chapter Fifteen

Organic Food, Food Allergies and Digestion

Although the largest sale of organic food is to mothers with young families, the various scare stories and promotional gimmicks of this huge industry have now induced many older people to buy their produce. It is, almost without exception, a huge waste of money.

The idea that food fed on rotting vegetation and the excreta of animals is somehow 'healthy' can be traced back to Victorian times, although in more recent years it has been exploited by the Soil Association and other 'back-to-nature' pressure groups. It is told that Prince Albert insisted that the waste from the toilets and the kitchens at Osborne House on the Isle of Wight should be used to fertilise the vegetable garden. Whether this was the source of the typhoid fever from which he died is open to conjecture, but the disease is only spread from consuming untreated faeces.

Today, pressure groups, including his descendants, spread the idea that there is something inherently beneficial in produce cultivated using manure and decaying vegetable matter as a fertiliser. There is not. They suggest that unless we eat organic food we will be poisoned by chemicals and our children are likely to suffer from all sorts of allergies, may become dyslexic or die of cancer. The method used to spread their message is similar to that used by Victorian missionaries in darkest Africa, where they scared the natives with tales of damnation and famine unless they embraced their particular belief.

A recent television programme (*Tonight with Trevor McDonald*, ITV, 30 September 2006) suggested that toxic chemicals, such as dioxins, are accumulating in our blood and could cause an 'epidemic of cancer'. The chemicals concerned are present in the blood of anyone who has been near a bonfire or eaten fatty fish. The concentrations are so low that even if they were a hundred times higher they would pose no risk. There is a far greater risk to health from pathogenic bacteria originating from manure contaminating organic produce. Spinach contaminated with *E coli* has recently caused an outbreak of fatal poisoning in America.

The principal message of the organic zealots is that chemicals are bad for you. They ignore the obvious fact that all food is composed of chemicals. As Anthony Trewavas, professor of plant biochemistry at the University of Edinburgh, has pointed out (*Times*, 27 September 2006), many natural chemicals are more toxic and carcinogenic in the concentrations found in nature than any chemicals used in conventional farming. Some are known to cause congenital malformations. There is no advantage in organic fertiliser. Plants can take in nutrition only through their root system, where they absorb a solution of chemicals dissolved in water. It does not matter whether the chemicals come from a plastic bag or from the breakdown of rotting organic waste – the plants cannot tell the difference.

What, then, of the chemicals used to prevent diseases caused by fungi and insects? The commonly used pesticides have a short half-life; that is, their concentration is rapidly reduced to a minimal concentration. Although minute amounts may still be detectable some days later, it is in such a small, picogram (that's one million millionth of a gram) concentration, that it needs the most sensitive chemical analysis to detect its presence. As far as I can gather, there has not been a single case of any person suffering from any clinically recognised complaint that has been attributed to any of these chemicals, taken in food from a normal uncontaminated source.

We know the symptoms of poisoning by these pesticides, as they have frequently been used as a means of attempting suicide, especially in Asia. There have also been unfortunate cases of them finding their way into prepared foods when sacks of pesticide and rice have been stored together. The symptoms they cause are watering eyes, salivation, gut cramps and diarrhoea, twitching of muscles and, if the dose is large, muscle weakness. They do not cause mental deterioration, skin rashes, cancer or loss of memory.

Many farmers in Asia are exposed year in, year out to high levels of these chemicals as they ignore safety guidelines and spray their crops for hours on end. They do not commonly suffer from allergies, they are not sterile and their brain is unaffected. They very occasionally suffer from muscle weakness.

The Food Standards Agency strictly controls the levels of all chemical pesticides in food. The maximum permitted level is one-hundredth of that which causes the first symptoms in the most susceptible animal. Even this tiny amount is usually found only on the outside of vegetables and fruit, allowing it to be washed away, unless a systemic pesticide has been used.

There is no evidence that any chemical used in the production of our food causes any harm. What, then, about additives? Many foods, especially prepared foods and sweets, contain chemicals that are added either to prolong the food's shelf life or to add flavour or colour. There is a vast number of these chemicals, all with *e* in front of their description, on labels. The *e* merely denoted their acceptance as safe and fit for the purpose by the EU. Most of them are naturally occurring chemicals such as vitamin C (ascorbic acid) and citric acid and sodium glutamate (found in mother's milk). It has been suggested that a few of the chemicals used as colouring may cause hyperexcitability in susceptible children, although there is little scientific evidence to support this contention.

There have been several trials to test the value of organic crops as opposed to more conventionally farmed foods. The most scientific, independent trial was the Boarded Barns Farm trial in Essex. Although the control land was conventionally farmed, wide boarders were left around the fields. The trial lasted five years, during which time the quality of the produce (independently assessed), the amount produced per hectare, the quality of the soil and the biodiversity were assessed. There was judged to be no difference in the quality of the produce but the organic yield was only a little over a half of the conventionally farmed yield. The biodiversity and the quality of the food were about the same but the organically farmed soil was judged to be less favourable from the second year on. It is because of the poor yields that organic produce is about 40 per cent more expensive than its counterpart. It has no advantages. It is a waste of money.

Organic meat is similarly indistinguishable from the meat of well-farmed animals. Organic chickens are fed a diet of 80 per cent organic food for the first six weeks only; after that time they eat what they like and are still labelled as 'organic'. They are reared in a manner that is certainly preferable to battery animals, but they lack the freedom of free-range birds.

There is absolutely no evidence that organic clothing is any different from any clothing not labelled as organic. It is an expensive nonsense. There are more potential allergens in natural products than in artificial ones.

The success of organic produce is testament to the power of marketing and the persuasiveness of fear. The selling of organic food has seen fear triumph over common sense. The exploitation of these fears by various pressure groups is reminiscent of the patent-medicine scandal exposed by the American journalist Norman Hapgood in 1905, who blamed advertising 'bunco men' (a US term for swindlers) for selling $75 million worth of useless, and in some cases dangerous, remedies to a gullible public. There is no sensible reason to pay extra for a product that is no better for you than any other. Indeed, organic food has a shorter shelf life, deteriorates more rapidly than conventional products and is more likely to from suffer bacterial contamination.

'We've never left anyone behind on our tours.'

Chapter Sixteen

Holidays and Travel

Retirement offers the freedom to fulfil one's dreams of travelling the world, exploring exotic places and engaging in sports and events previously impossible because of the restrictions imposed by a working life.

Many people look forward to marking their initiation into their new life by doing what they want, when they want to; to many this involves going on the holiday of a lifetime. It might be the chance to fulfil a long-held dream of a voyage around the world, a trip to visit relatives in Australia or a trek to the Himalayas. This often means weeks or months away from home. It is an ideal preface to a new life and should not be put off. Too often these yearnings are delayed and some unforeseen event or illness intervenes so that this wish never gets fulfilled and all that is left is regrets.

A fabulous, longed-for holiday can be the ideal time to consider the future and to decide upon your priorities in the years ahead. It shouldn't be regarded as a means of escape from the realities of life or embarked on as a cure for depression or an attempt to escape from a particular problem. In these circumstances it's doomed to be a disappointment. Once the holiday's over, it will become clear that the problem hasn't been solved and the depression is likely to return.

The over-fifties now make up a huge proportion of those travelling for leisure; they outnumber and outspend the family holiday travellers. They have prolonged the peak travel seasons. Today, in many resorts, the January and February periods are often as busy as the summer holidays or the run-up to Christmas.

Those recently retired usually seek longer breaks than those with a regular holiday allotment. They seek travel that takes them to places or sites of interest rather than places of hedonistic leisure. Often they prefer to travel from place to place as part of a tour group rather than as a family. Those less fit or older tend to favour less adventurous holidays, a trend that has contributed to the boom in the cruise-ship industry.

An alternative is to make a once-only investment in a

time-share or holiday property bond. The popularity of a shared ownership of a holiday flat or villa abroad has resulted in a boom in co-ownership developments in places such as Madeira, Spain, Greece and Turkey. In general, time-shares are less flexible than property holiday bonds. Investment in these companies allows access to villas all over the world, once the initial investment has been made. The best schemes offer excellent opportunities for regular cheap holidays abroad; the worst involve purchasers in continuous expense without any hope of a return on their investment. Always seek advice and pay attention to the fine print before signing up to these schemes. Never make this sort of investment on an impulse under pressure from a salesman when on holiday.

With the advent of cheap air travel no place is too far or too remote for the intrepid traveller and the effort is often rewarded by sights and experiences that were in previous generations available only to the very wealthy. However, travel does carry certain hazards, especially as we get older and actuarially more 'at risk' than when young. It is as well to make provision for any problems before embarking on a visit overseas.

Endemic diseases

Endemic diseases are present in certain countries. Malaria

is present in the mosquitoes of most of Africa and poses a significant risk, except in South Africa and some parts of Botswana. It is a potential risk in much of Southeast Asia and India, where the seawater mosquito also carries the virus causing dengue fever, or 'break-back fever' as it has come to be known. Anyone travelling to Asia or Africa should consult their GP or telephone one of the help lines. There is one associated with MASTA (Medical Advisory Service for Travellers Abroad), one with the School of Tropical Medicine and another with British Airways (see Useful Addresses).

Before visiting some developing countries and in the outlying parts of other countries where the integrity of the fresh water supply is in doubt, you're advised to have jabs against typhoid fever and hepatitis. When travelling to remote places and to areas with a high rate of HIV infection, it is sensible to consider taking a pack containing a sterile syringe and needles.

There are various different medical regimes that offer a high degree of protection against the malarial parasite. One should check which is recommended for the particular area to be visited as the resistance to some anti-malarial drugs is now common. Lariam, the proprietary name of mefloquine hydrochloride, a drug that offers very wide protection, has major disadvantages in the older person, who may hallucinate, become acutely depressed or develop muscle spasm or fits. For those who are intolerant of chloroquine and Paludrine (proguanil) medication, Malarone offers a good, if less effective, alternative.

Although there is no perfect insect repellent, those containing 40 per cent DEET are recommended. If going on a camping or tented safari holiday it's advisable to carry a DDT spray for use inside the tent to deter insects and mosquitoes. Insect repellents are especially important at dusk and dawn, when mosquitoes are most active. The so-called natural insect repellents are relatively ineffective.

One of the benefits of cruising for older people is that their medical needs are well catered for on most cruise ships. This does not necessarily ensure that their health may not be at risk. Infective viral enteritis is endemic in a few cruise ships and it is not unknown for passengers who disembark for a few hours to visit a place of interest to return home with malaria because they have failed to take antimalarial drugs. This is especially likely to happen if the visit has taken place at twilight.

As people live longer and more active lives it is likely that more will spend a greater proportion of their time travelling once they retire. They should not be put off by the occasional story of an unfortunate mishap. The vast majority of tours and cruises are very well organised and offer a good opportunity to see other parts of the world at a reasonable price and with a minimum of inconvenience. Every new experience helps in preventing the tendency to restrict your interest to the familiar as you get older.

Safe eating and drinking

In many countries the tap water is unsafe for drinking by a casual visitor. It is advisable always to play safe and drink bottled water, and to carry some water-purification tablets to add to water used for cleaning your teeth. In areas where the water may be contaminated by pathogenic bacteria, safe eating means avoiding anything that has not been cooked or peeled. Fresh, well-cooked meat and fish are safe but shellfish should be avoided. Only well-cooked vegetables should be eaten. Salads can be dangerous even if they have been washed in chlorinated water. Fruit that has been peeled is safe. Try to avoid buffet meals, as it is not unknown for food to be reheated and recycled through buffets. The food displayed at buffets is also open to contamination by flies and other insects.

The two main types of food poisoning are enterotoxin poisoning, which causes a short-lived painful episode of diarrhoea and vomiting associated with gut cramps, and infective enteritis, which causes prolonged gut cramps and diarrhoea together with a mild fever. Infective enteritis occurs from eating food infected with pathogenic bacteria.

The first type of poisoning is self-limiting. Once a firm diagnosis of the second is made it should be treated with a drug such as Imodium, to lessen the diarrhoea, and the antibiotic ciprofloxacin to treat the infection. If it does not improve in three or four days, seek medical advice. In both types of food poisoning, it is important to replace any fluid and salt lost as a result of the diarrhoea.

It is probable that a suntan provides the most effective sun block for the skin. There is no scientifically proven reason for avoiding sunshine. But sunburn is dangerous and great care should be taken to avoid sudden, excessive exposure to the tropical sun, especially if you are fair-skinned. Heat stroke is due to an excessive loss of fluid and salt, in the form of sweat, as the body attempts to lose heat and lower the core temperature. It is the intense vasodilatation (widening of blood vessels) in the skin that gives rise to the shivering associated with this condition. The dehydration due to the loss of water and salt causes the dizziness and headache. It is much more likely to occur if the skin has been overexposed to the sun. Baldness increases the risk of overexposure to the sun. It is sensible to wear a hat when the sun is at its hottest.

Insurance

Before embarking on overseas travel, especially if it is to a region poorly served by medical specialists and hospitals, it is essential to make sure you are covered against any medical expenses. Some private medical insurers cover overseas travel as part of their care package, while others cover only emergency consultations and evacuation to the UK. Travel-insurance policies usually cover the cost of medical emergency, but it is sensible to study the small print to make sure there are no exclusions that may apply to you.

Many of these policies are age-limited. The cost often increases considerably the older you are, and insurance cover may be denied, by some insurers, to anyone over seventy or seventy-five. Some companies will give cover up to the age of eighty but it is exceptional to find medical insurance available to the over-eighties. To travel to a remote destination without medical cover is like playing Russian roulette.

The situation for the traveller within the EU is different. Provided you have a European Health Insurance Card (EHIC), any charge for medical emergencies will be heavily discounted or completely reimbursed, depending upon the insurance system in that country. This also applies to Switzerland. (The EHIC is available to all UK citizens. See Appendix C, 'Useful Addresses'.)

Another problem often complained about by the older traveller is the inability to hire a car in some countries due to the refusal of some insurers to offer cover to those over sixty-nine. This applies to many hire-car companies in Ireland and mainland Europe, although not in France or Spain. You should tell the hire company your age when booking a car to prevent a holiday being ruined when you find you can't pick up a car at your destination, in spite of it having been pre-booked.

Deep-vein thrombosis

Air travel has been incriminated as a cause of deep-vein thrombosis (DVT) and pulmonary emboli. The risk is similar whether you travel by air or coach: it is related to sitting relatively still for over four hours. Older people are at an increased risk because their blood is slightly stickier and the blood flow in their legs is reduced to a greater extent than in a young person. So it's imperative that you take sensible precautions to reduce the risk.

Keep up your blood volume by drinking fluids freely before the flight. It is sensible to add salt so as to maintain as high a circulating volume as possible, and take a low-dose (75mg) tablet of aspirin before boarding. Wriggling the toes and pumping the calf muscles helps to promote blood flow in the legs, but getting up and strolling along the aisle is even better. The use of elastic stockings has been advocated. They may help reduce the ankle swelling that occurs in older people during a long flight as well as reducing the risk of DVT.

A large intake of alcohol (over three units) should be avoided, but there is no reason not to drink a glass of wine with meals.

'For heaven's sake...you're going to have to switch
out of this work mode.'

Chapter Seventeen

Opportunities in Retirement

Opportunities for work

For those recently retired it is fairly easy to find out what part-time or full-time employment opportunities are available. Unfortunately, it's more difficult to find an employer willing to use your services when you're over fifty-five. Recent employment legislation bans job discrimination on the basis of age, but it doesn't seem to have opened up the job market. There are various reasons why this should be so, but the most intractable one is that many managers and senior executives find the presence of someone older, and possibly more experienced than themselves, a threat to their own position.

This means that only relatively menial posts are made

available and someone who has recently retired from a responsible job may find this difficult to accept. It is easier to find posts that provide work for only one or two days a week in the various government bodies set up to scrutinise the effectiveness of their public initiatives. These posts are never well paid. Jobs are occasionally advertised in the national or local newspapers or at job centres, but, unless you have a particular skill that is in short supply, well-paid employment is often difficult to find.

Voluntary work

It is one of the shortcomings of successive governments that the very real desire of recently retired people to help in the public sector has never been addressed. There are thousands of fit, energetic retirees who would like to serve the community in a voluntary capacity, on a part-time basis. Meeting this need would not only help the community but also help many to come to terms with the feeling that they are being 'put out to grass' when they retire.

It is a 'twice-blessed' situation that could easily be met by a national register of part-time voluntary posts. It would then be up to a health authority, a school, a community centre, a sports facility and the social services to register the kinds of jobs that need to be done and the skills they require. Such a register could be accessed on the Internet.

Without any central or local register, it is necessary to look for these posts in one of several disparate places. Few of the lists that can be accessed are likely to be complete. At the moment you have to search in many places and to keep a constant watch for posts to be advertised. The Retired and Senior Volunteer Programme (see Appendix, 'Useful Addresses') offers a selection of opportunities to help in the local community, but its services seem to be directed at elderly retirees and those who need something to do in order to get them out of the confines of their homes.

Enquiries about volunteer posts can be made at the local library, but this facility does not appear to be used to advertise the opportunities that are available to work in a specialist capacity for the various government agencies. Some town councils do have a volunteers' bureau, which acts as a sorting house for those needing help. Some job centres and Citizens' Advice Bureaux also carry a list of voluntary jobs. Local newspapers often carry requests for voluntary help but they frequently require a specific skill or ethnic background. National newspapers may carry advertisements, in their not-for-profit advertisement sections, from various regional bodies that require people to serve on their statutory committees.

Many schools use volunteers to help, on a one-to-one basis, with children who are having difficulty learning to read or add up. Hospitals often welcome help from car drivers who will take disabled patients to and from treatment. There is a need for people to read to children in hospital and to blind people. Meals-on-wheels organisations carry out a unique service in the community and are often grateful for volunteers. Prison visitors are needed, as are people to check on the welfare of persons in detention.

There are a variety of statutory bodies and various government tribunals that require a lay representation on their board. The problem is finding out which body requires volunteers at any particular time. For people with some managerial skills, such as accountants and lawyers, Reach, a charity for those looking for voluntary work, offers a register of various charities that require trustees or managers.

The hurdles that have to be overcome before we can find out how to help out in the community are a source of considerable frustration and explain why many people find a post by talking to friends who work in the public sector and who know what needs to be done and whom to approach.

One word of caution: although these voluntary jobs are without pay or expenses, it is common to find it necessary to have to pay yourself to have the positive vetting of your character required for many of these posts.

Further learning

Once they retire, many people fancy taking on a further-education course. There is an immense variety of courses, from learning to play the piano and philosophy to sculpture and metalworking, on offer in schools and institutes of further learning. Sadly, it is not unknown for some of them to collapse after a few weeks because of dwindling support. Inevitably, the better courses, with the most professional teachers, will be in the urban centres. These courses used to be very cheap, but in the present financial climate, schools have to meet tight budgets and the cost of further education has increased considerably. It's a good idea to try to speak to someone on the course before you enrol and pay the tuition fee, since the standards of instruction vary greatly.

When selecting any course, bear in mind that any study that puts a premium on memory, such as history or a new language, may prove too difficult as one gets older and it becomes increasingly difficult to remember names and dates.

The Open University offers excellent tuition leading to a higher degree or qualification. These courses are always well prepared and exacting. They are not to be embarked upon unless you're willing to put aside at least two days a week for the course work. Some of the courses may be quite expensive.

The University of the Third Age, or U3A, started in France

as an opportunity for people who had a university degree to gain a higher degree or to learn a new subject after they retired. In this country they are open to all. The nature of the U3As varies greatly from place to place. In some they bring retired people together for social events, such as bridge and domestic pursuits, but in most they present lectures and courses of study that are largely educational.

Courses on current affairs, economics and legal developments are regularly presented at the meetings. You can pick and choose the subjects that interest you. Some are very socially oriented and include visits to places of interest. Since their members run them, it is *their* wishes that set the tone of the meetings. They are inexpensive.

There has been an explosion in the number of book clubs that meet regularly throughout the year. The local library often has information on the organiser of the one in your area. Bridge clubs often advertise for new members in local papers, although some are attached to the U3A. Sports and exercise facilities, some subsidised by the council, are available in many areas. Fitness classes and Pilates are offered by some boroughs. You can usually find details in your local library.

There are very many music societies and amateur orchestras, especially in the larger towns. Details are usually advertised in the local library. Lectures and political meetings are generally well advertised in local newspapers.

The needs of the retiree have been met in many different ways. London is fortunate in having places like the Royal Institute, which presents lectures on a wide variety of scientific subjects three times a week. There are lectures at the Geographical Society, Imperial College, University College and the Royal Society. Many rehearsals by National orchestras, opera and ballet companies are open to the public. There are frequent talks given by actors or producers at the National Theatre, explaining the details of a particular theatrical production.

It is sensible when confronted with this plethora of choice to decide the area of your interest and to centre your attention on that subject. You are more likely to become involved and to form meaningful relationships once you develop an expertise in a particular subject.

There are plenty of opportunities to widen your intellectual horizon once you've retired. Failure to take advantage of these is frequently due to inertia or a reluctance to initiate something new. It is easier to embrace a new experience with a partner or friend. A reluctance to take advantage of the opportunities for broadening your intellectual horizon can be a symptom of depression. When you retire, it is essential to take steps to organise a lifestyle that embraces new opportunities that are both fulfilling and enjoyable.

'Your father made out a will in his own hand...
the trouble is none of us can read it.'

Chapter Eighteen

Money Matters: Some of the Problems

The opportunities for enjoying retirement are inevitably dependent upon outside factors, including family considerations, good health and financial constraints. To those approaching retirement, the sudden change in financial status and the possibility that they may one day have to finance residential care for themselves or their spouse introduces an unwelcome uncertainty into their plans for retirement.

A recent survey found that about 60 per cent of those retiring had no idea as to how to provide for such eventualities, while a minority refused to contemplate the prospect of needing to provide for a catastrophic event that would necessitate residential care. Fortunately, only a minority of those recently retired will be required to fund a place in a care home but, unless they have made provision for such an eventuality, the cost will have to be met by selling the family home.

State help is very limited unless the placement in the care home is deemed to be medically essential or the person's total assets are less than £21,000. It is because the advent of this necessity seems such a distant possibility when people retire that very few make provision for it in their plans, hoping that, if necessary, the state will look after them.

So, prudent financial planning for retirement should not only look at present needs but also allow, as far as possible, for unexpected future events.

Sensible and realistic planning is essential for those approaching retirement. It must be sufficiently flexible to meet any fluctuations in the financial scene. It should not only look to your immediate needs and allow for unexpected expenses, but also produce income to pay for the occasional indulgences that add zest to life. It is reasonable to maximise your income at this stage in your life rather than to seek to accumulate capital. Because inheritance tax will take 40 per cent of any residual estate (see Appendix A, which deals with legal matters, including tax), it is pointless to deny yourself any pleasure in order to leave money in your will to your children. You should take comfort in the thought that for every pound you spend you are denying the taxman 40p.

Not everyone's needs will be the same when they retire. The size of pensions will vary and most will have capital tied up in their home. People should think carefully and take advice, before realising the value of this asset. Those with money to invest need to consider their priorities carefully before committing their reserve. Money lost at this stage of your life is not easily recouped. For this reason it is a good idea to seek expert advice before taking any irrevocable steps.

Decisions shouldn't be taken lightly. Without an overall plan and sound advice expensive mistakes are likely to be made. It is for this reason that I have asked an experienced expert, Roger Parkes, independent financial adviser, to outline the essentials of a sensible approach to financial planning in retirement. You can see his advice in Appendix B.

"One day son, all this will not be yours!"

Epilogue

Happy Talk

My publishers suggested that at the end of this book, a large part of which is devoted to telling the story of the changes that occur as one gets older, there should perhaps be a more upbeat message, a note of encouraging optimism, such as a list of the achievements made by those long past their retirement age or of the records set by octogenarians. However, once I started researching these fields I ran into the problem of determining who could actually be described as 'old' and what distinguished their exploits from those of younger people.

For example, is my eighty-year-old friend who, in his words, 'strolled up Mount Everest', really old? I am sure he does not consider himself as such. He is still very active in the field of research. The only problem he attributed to his age was the difficulty he had getting out of his sleeping bag after lying on the ground in the tent, following a night in the freezing cold!

Are the eight seventy-five to eighty-year-old sailors, who moor their boat on the same pontoon as I do, old? They are as ready as a younger person to sail off to distant parts – and often do.

There are those like the late American medical scientist Francis Foldes, who would demonstrate his prowess at water skiing by performing on one ski well into his eighties. He would have rightly been insulted to have been considered 'old'.

Can one really describe my eighty-year-old colleagues who play tennis, go sail-boarding and who fence as 'old'?

Then there is the ninety-year-old who has just completed his second Open University degree, the politicians who continue to wield power well into their eighties and those over-eighties in the performing arts who continue to receive the plaudits of the critics. What is it that distinguishes them from the rest of us? It is evident that neither chronological age alone nor the biblical suggestion that person's life span is three score years and ten allows us a sensible definition of the elderly. Few of these people are 'super-fit', or free of the problems that I have described in this book, which beset us all as we get older. The main difference is that they *do not accept* that they are old.

My memories of my parents are that they were 'old'. When my granddaughter asks me if I rode in a hansom cab when I was young and whether Grandma wore crinolines, I realise that in her eyes I am old; but the person I am does not feel old when he wakes up in the morning or when he is dining with friends. It is the perception that we're getting on in years that inhibits us from trying to climb our own particular Everest. It is a perception that is becoming more and more out of tune with actuality.

There has been an amazing change in what constitutes old age over the past fifty years, and we have been slow to alter our attitudes so as to come to terms with the changes that science, medicine and public-health measures have achieved. No longer does a greater life span mean more time to suffer, in the way it would have done fifty years ago. By stopping smoking and by cleaning up the air we breathe we have reduced the incidence of the pulmonary diseases, emphysema and bronchitis, to a point where they are barely visible on the medical horizon. The control of blood pressure by drugs has reduced the incidence of catastrophic strokes by about 30 per cent; and, by the better treatment of those strokes that do occur, we can now greatly reduce their disabling effects. The incidence of heart attacks is falling all over the world (in spite of a generally higher intake of fats) and coronary-artery disease, causing angina and a limitation of exercise, can now be treated effectively in most patients without recourse to surgery.

Joint-replacement surgery is now so good that having a new hip or knee merely means a couple of weeks off the golf course. The overall effect has been almost as revolutionary as the increase in life expectancy itself. The difference is that we have been even slower to appreciate and utilise this new potential. Today, a longer life belies the definition of ageing as 'a progressive impairment of function', or, as John Grimley Evans[2] put it, 'a longer time dying'. Raymond Tallis,[3] a distinguished geriatrician, has pointed out that today those who live to be eighty-five or over actually need less time being looked after by a carer than those who die in their late sixties. The number of days spent in hospital by someone dying at ninety is now only a little over double that of someone dying at half that age, at forty-five.

Tallis suggests that medical advances have not only

2 John Grimley Evans (1998), 'Ageing', in Marshall Marinker and Michael Peckham (eds), *Clinical Futures* (BMJ Publications).
3 Raymond Tallis (2004), *Hippocratic Oaths* (Atlantic Books).

postponed death, so that we live longer, but that they have also postponed many of the illnesses that we used to associate with old age. In all probability, this is a trend that will continue. There is a reasonable expectation that drugs will be developed, in the near future, to reduce the effects of memory loss and that stem-cell treatments will be available to alleviate the effects of Parkinson's disease.

The real message that needs to be appreciated and it is truly one of optimism is that, although most people in their seventies would have been in need of full- or part-time care because of their disabilities fifty years ago, today 85–90 per cent of people are fully mobile and active well into their eighties. Fifty years ago a study revealed that more than 30 per cent of women in America over sixty-five could be described as 'functionally disabled'; today it is likely that fewer than 10 per cent of those over eighty-five would fall into this category.

This is the real story of the third age and it is cause for considerable optimism. Ageing is the perception of us made by others. As we get older, we see ourselves as more mature, but just as able as younger people, even if there are some physical constraints that impair our competitiveness. As we get older, the only real limits to our aspirations and to our activities are those we impose upon ourselves.

Appendix A

It's the Law: A Look at Legal Matters

BY REGINALD GLICK, SOLICITOR, MEMBER OF
THE RETIREMENT TRUST

As we grow older, we may find ourselves in one of two positions. We may either become a carer, looking after a spouse or other relative who has become mentally or physically frail, or we may need to be cared for by others.

A word on terminology first. I refer to *spouse* a lot in this chapter, but this term will also refer to a civil partner under the Civil Partnership Act 2004, which came into force in December 2005.

The traditional method of giving someone else the authority to deal with our financial affairs, if we are too weak or do not want to be bothered, was to give them what is known as a *power of attorney*. This allowed them to act on our behalf with our automatic authority. This type of ordinary power of attorney was automatically revoked if the donor became mentally incapacitated. As a result, when one came to sell one's parent's house when he or she moved into a sheltered accommodation or a care home, one might be faced with a problem if the solicitor believed the parent had gone into the home because of mental incapacity.

To remedy this potentially difficult situation a new *enduring* power of attorney became available in 1986. This enabled someone to whom such a power of attorney had been granted to continue to act in spite of suspected mental incapacity of the donor. Obviously, there had to be safeguards against it being misused.

Enduring powers of attorney

The first thing to consider before giving an enduring power of attorney is the person to whom are you going to give this power. The most obvious choice will be your husband, wife or civil partner. The next will be your children, but then you have to decide whether, if you have more than one, you will give the power to just one of them or to more. One may live round the corner, one in the USA, and one you may not see from one year's end to the other. If you give them the power 'jointly', they can exercise it only if they are in unanimous agreement, which means that any one can veto the decisions of the others.

Alternatively, if you give it to them 'jointly and severally', then each one can act individually and whichever one gets in first will have successfully bound the others. If you do not have a spouse, partner or children, you will probably choose a close relative or a very trusted close friend, failing which you may ask your solicitor or accountant to act on your behalf.

You can make the power of attorney capable of being operated right away, although this does not stop you, while you are still able, from acting on your own behalf, but whatever your attorney does in your name will bind you legally. The alternative is to say that you do not want it to be capable of being operated by the attorney until such time as it has been registered with the Public Guardianship Office, part of the Court of Protection.

The Court of Protection is a Division of the High Court of Justice and it regulates the affairs of mentally disadvantaged persons. Any questions arising about what can or cannot be done under an enduring power of attorney are decided by the court. It also has the power, under certain circumstances, to make a will for a mentally disadvantaged person.

An enduring power of attorney has to be made on a

special form. You can obtain one from any good firm of stationers and the pack contains the information you need about how they have to be signed and by whom.

It is the recipient of the power, the attorney (the *donee*), who has the responsibility of registering it with the Court of Protection. The court asks that the donee should register it as soon as they feel that the donor is becoming mentally impaired. No evidence of mental impairment has to be lodged with the power itself, but the safeguards against misuse come from the *notices*, which have to be given to certain persons at that time. The donor has to be given notice so that they can object, stating that they are still perfectly hale and hearty and that they do not believe that they are becoming mentally impaired. Once this has been achieved, notice has to be given to everybody in 'three classes of persons who have a relationship to the donor'.

There is a list and an order of priority. The first are spouses, then children (including adopted but not stepchildren), brothers and sisters (including those of the half-blood), children's widows or widowers, grandchildren and so on down to cousins. If any of the persons in any of the three classes thinks that the donee is unsuitable to be the attorney, they can object within the time limited by the notice. If there is a real dispute about suitability it will be decided by the Court of Protection, which has the power to revoke an enduring power if it thinks the circumstances are unsuitable.

An attorney under an enduring power cannot do exactly what they like with the property of the donor. Money that belongs to the donor, e.g. from the sale of a property, must be invested and used for the benefit of the donor. The attorney can do whatever the donor customarily used to do. For example, if the donor used to give each of his nephews and nieces presents of £100 every Christmas, the attorney can continue the practice, but anything else requires the sanction of the Court of Protection, to whom the attorney remains accountable.

An enduring power of attorney enables the donee to deal only with the donor's financial affairs. It does not enable them to deal with health matters, nor, for example, to make a will for the donor. From April 2007 there will be a new type of power of attorney, called a *lasting power of attorney*, which *will* enable health matters to be dealt with by the donee. It will not be dissimilar to the enduring power, but will have additional rights and duties attached to it. It will no longer be possible to grant an enduring power after the new form of attorney comes into force, although all those powers that have been granted up to that time will continue to be valid.

Living wills

Until April 2007 the law will not recognise what are commonly called *living wills*, by which people state, for example, that they do not wish to be resuscitated in certain circumstances. After that date, *advance decisions to refuse treatment* will be capable of being given by adults. Detailed wishes can be spelled out, including what can be done if at the time the person lacks the ability to give the necessary consent, as well as what is not to be done. The decision can be withdrawn at any time, while the person is still competent to withdraw it, and, if the provisions of a lasting power of attorney confer powers on the attorney to give or refuse consent to treatment that conflicts with a previously expressed decision, the lasting power of attorney will prevail. Where matters of actual life and death are concerned, there must be a statement in writing that the decision is to apply even though the life of the person who made the provisions is at risk. The statement has to be witnessed, like a will, although only one witness will be required.

Jointly held property

Many people do not realise that there can be very different consequences stemming from the legal way that a property that they share is held. Apart from anything else, it can affect the amount of inheritance tax payable. Leaving aside things such as spouse exemption, inheritance tax will be payable on the value of a deceased person's share of a property, however it is held. The property itself may, however, go in a different direction from what was expected.

Property is either *movable* or *immovable*; immovable for this purpose really means land and buildings, while movable covers everything else. If you have money in a joint bank account, a joint share or deposit account in a building society, stock exchange securities in joint names or joint life-assurance policies, they will, unless they have been set up on specifically different terms, generally pass automatically to the survivor. It is a good idea to maintain a joint bank account, with a modest sum in it, which you never use, so that, on the death of the first to die, the survivor has immediate access to some money in that account, which he or she can obtain without having to wait until a grant of probate or letters of administration have been obtained.

When it comes to land and buildings, however, whether freehold or leasehold, there are two ways of holding them in co-ownership, called respectively *joint tenancy* and *tenancy in common*. In the case of husbands and wives, before divorce became so fashionable and commonplace, it was very usual for property being purchased by them to be put in their names as joint tenants. The result is that in such cases the survivor automatically takes the property on the death of the first to die. The succession is automatic, by operation of the law. You cannot leave your half-share to anyone else in your will – at the moment you die, the share of the property that was yours passes over to the survivor automatically.

Conversely, if you are a tenant in common, you may leave your share to whomever you like and there is no automatic passing of it to the survivor. This may make things very awkward for the survivor, who may be required to give up possession of the property to satisfy the demands of the persons to whom you have left your share. To get round this problem, you can give your surviving co-tenant – usually your widow or widower or civil partner – the right to continue to live in the property during the remainder of their lifetime, but this will result in their being treated by the Inland Revenue, when they die, for inheritance tax purposes, as if they owned your share of the house as well as their own.

It is possible to exclude your share of the property from bearing an inheritance-tax liability on the death of your partner, but for this result it is necessary for the property to be held as tenants in common and not joint tenants, and for your will to contain very special provisions. If you want to take advantage of this possibility, you must consult your title deeds and make sure that you are indeed tenants in common and not joint tenants. If you do discover that you are joint tenants and not tenants in common and you want to alter the situation, you can do so during your lifetime by serving what is called a *notice of severance*, but you cannot do it through your will: by then it is too late.

Wills and intestacies

If you do not leave a will, the state will decide where your property will go when you die. A surviving spouse (including a civil partner) will receive a very limited amount. There is no right for a spouse automatically to receive everything and there is no such thing as a common-law spouse. There may be legislation in the future that will give partners and cohabitees greater rights, but at the moment the rights of such persons are extremely limited.

Under the general intestacy law, a surviving spouse gets the first £125,000 if there are children, the personal chattels and a life interest in (that is, the right to receive the income from) half of the remainder of the estate of the deceased. Today, that half may not take a surviving spouse very far. The children take the other half between them immediately, and the first half goes to them after the surviving spouse dies. This can cause great difficulties where the main asset is a house worth more than £125,000 and the children would like to get their hands on their immediate half share of the residue at once.

Even if there are no children, the spouse gets only the first £200,000 and a life interest in half the remainder. (These figures are revised at very infrequent intervals and may well be increased in 2007.) The deceased's parents or brothers and sisters or their issue will take the rest. Only if there are no parents or brothers or sisters or their issue will the surviving spouse take everything. If there is no surviving spouse, either, then other relatives come into the picture, right down to half-brothers and half-sisters of the deceased's parents and the issue of any deceased's half-uncle or half-aunt, and if there is no one at all then the estate will go to the Crown. However, the unenviable situation of a surviving spouse becomes evident even when there are only children or parents of the deceased to be dealt with, particularly if the matrimonial home is worth considerably more than the capital sum passing to the spouse.

For this reason it is essential to leave a will so that you can say, in the main, where and to whom you would like your property to pass. Bear in mind, however, that there may be certain restrictions on what you can do. Foreign property may well be subject to the laws of the country in which it is situated and some countries, for example France and Spain, will not let you simply disinherit your surviving spouses and children. You may be well advised to make a separate will of foreign property in the country in which it is situated.

Remember, too, that marriage (including entering into civil partnership) revokes a will and divorce affects anything in one's will concerning one's ex-spouse or former civil partner.

Your will has to be in writing and signed by you at its end, in the presence of two witnesses, who must be together at the time when you sign it or acknowledge your signature on it. Generally it is best if the three of you are together for all the time of the signing. If a beneficiary acts as a witness, the will will still be valid but as a witness they will be prevented from benefiting from the will. They will forfeit anything given to them by the will.

As with the power of attorney, you must decide who you want to be your executors. They will, however, have to act unanimously unless your will expressly says that the majority is to prevail. You will normally want such a provision only if you are creating trusts that are going to go on after the initial distribution of your estate. Your executors will realise your assets, pay your debts and funeral expenses and then pay any inheritance tax due. They have an obligation to distribute any legacies you have left and, finally, to dispose of the residue of your estate.

To avoid any ambiguities that may arise it is generally sensible to avoid a homemade will and to employ a solicitor to draw your will. The solicitor should make sure that you describe your property accurately, describe the beneficiaries and what they are to get accurately, and do not fall into any inheritance-tax traps. If you give someone 'the money in my bank account at the date of my death', it has to be made clear whether it includes money in the building society, and whether it is the only account you maintain. If you give £30,000 'between my sister, Rose, and her children in equal shares' and she has two children, do they each take £10,000 or does Rose take £15,000 and each of the children £7,500? If you leave your son 'my Ferrari' and you change the Ferrari the week before you die for a Lamborghini, will you be surprised that he gets neither the price you got for the Ferrari nor the Lamborghini? Worst of all, if you leave a million pounds and give a legacy of £250,000 to each of your two children and the residue to your spouse, in the belief that he or she will get half a million because the gift to your spouse will be free from inheritance tax, you will be mistaken. In these circumstances it is likely that the children will get their quarter-million pounds each, unless you said that their gifts were to bear their own tax, and the spouse (on 2006 rates of inheritance tax) would get only £360,000. This is because the whole of the inheritance tax of about £140,000 payable would come out of the residue left to the spouse.

Finally, if you made your will at home in simple language, and left everything to your spouse, and then to the children, would you be surprised to know that your spouse would be entitled to everything and the children to nothing? A solicitor might well point out these sorts of things to you, as well as how to avoid them.

Deeds of variation

There are a number of circumstances in which your will can be effectively rewritten after your death and the legacies that you gave can be varied. One of these is by a *deed of variation* (otherwise called a *deed of family arrangement*). If your bequests are relatively straightforward and do not involve complicated trusts or infant children (under eighteen years of age), the adult beneficiaries can get together and divide what has been left to them in a different way from that stated in your will. If those alterations mean that one gets more and one gets less, the one getting less would be making a gift to the one getting more and that might expose him or her to a liability both to capital-gains tax and inheritance tax if he/she did not survive for seven years from the making of the gift.

However, if the alterations are made within two years

from a person's death, the law allows them to be treated as if they had been part of the provisions of the testator's will and both capital-gains tax and inheritance tax may be saved.

If a husband, concerned primarily with his wife's security, were to leave her the whole of his estate, there would be no inheritance tax payable because gifts to spouses are exempt from inheritance tax. If she decided nearly two years afterwards that she did not want or need all this, and made a gift of some of it to her children, she would, were it not for this legislation, have to wait seven years before that gift became free from inheritance tax. But with the legislation the gift can be treated as if it had been in the testator's will and a considerable amount of capital-gains tax and inheritance tax may be saved.

These changes to your will, perhaps involving gifts, are voluntary. The next way in which your wishes expressed in your will may be changed retrospectively, after your death, is not voluntary!

The Inheritance (Provision for Family and Dependants) Act 1975

There are a number of persons for whom the law requires you to make reasonable provision after you die and, if you do not, they can apply to the court for provision to be made for them from your estate. They include spouses and ex-spouses – and, now, civil partners – children, dependants, people to whose support you have been contributing, and anyone with whom you have been living as man and wife or civil partner in the same household for the last two years of your life.

'Reasonable provision' means different things in different cases. For a spouse, it means what he or she might have been awarded by the court if there had been a divorce on the day of the death. In the light of some of the recent Divorce Court awards to spouses, this could be a great deal of money. Civil partners are now on an equal footing. For all others, it means a sum, which may be capital or income, or both, that is sufficient to provide reasonable maintenance, which means living neither in luxury nor in poverty but at a level that is reasonable in the claimant's circumstances and suitable to his or her station in life. This can amount to a substantial amount of money and embrace, in the case of a young child, the cost of education and, in the case of an older person, the fact that they may well need medical care and attention in the later years of their life.

The court will look at everything but, although it must take into account all the other legitimate claims there may be on the estate from all other persons, and it can take into account to some extent your reasons for not leaving the applicant more – or perhaps anything at all – there appears to be no necessity for the claimant to exhibit any moral claim to be entitled to your generosity. The result may well be that you cannot now cut off your children without a shilling, no matter how beastly they may have been to you.

Inheritance tax

Benjamin Franklin once said that in life only two things are certain: death and taxes. From time to time it is suggested that inheritance tax may be abolished, but at the moment of writing, in 2006, it is still with us. One part of it operates on your estate, but for this purpose your estate comprises not only what you leave when you die, but also whatever you may have given away in the seven years prior to your death. The subject is now so complex that it is possible to deal with it only in the most general outline.

There are some exceptions to the rule. Gifts to spouses or civil partners are exempt. There are reliefs given to agricultural property and business property, for example shares in a family trading company. Gifts to charity and political parties are exempt. Everyone can give away £3,000 to anyone annually, and £6,000 if a year is missed, as well as £250 annually to as many other people as they like. Each parent and grandparent can give £5,000 and £2,500 respectively to anyone who is getting married.

Finally, if you have sufficient surplus income, year in and year out, to be able to give some of it away regularly, so that it becomes part of your normal expenditure without in the least affecting your own standard of living, you can give away as much of that as you wish.

Inheritance tax now operates as a lifetime gift tax as well as a tax payable on death. Unless your lifetime gift is an absolute one, i.e. without any strings, or trusts, attached to it, when you simply have to survive the seven years before it falls out of liability to tax, or it falls within one of the exceptions – for example life interests to spouses – you will generally have to pay tax at 20 per cent on it forthwith, and if you die within seven years another 20 per cent will be taken then. This will bring it up to the 40 per cent that is the normal rate of inheritance tax. In addition, while any trust affecting it remains in existence, it will bear tax of up to 6 per cent on its current value every ten years.

These rates of tax may be changed, of course, but the rate at the end of 2006 payable on a person's estate, including the lifetime gifts mentioned, is 40 per cent on everything except the first £285,000, which is taxable at 0 per cent and is called the *nil-rate band*. This nil-rate-band amount is supposed to increase each year by the rate of inflation, but the Chancellor of the Exchequer has said that for 2007/8 it will be increased to £300,000 and by 2010 it will be £325,000.

Lifetime gifts that you make, unless you survive the seven years, will be using up your nil-rate band, but on the other hand you can make *absolute* gifts in your lifetime up to the value of the nil-rate band at the time, without having to pay any tax immediately. If your lifetime gifts go over that value, and you die within the seven years, you get some tapering of the tax payable, depending on whether you have survived the making of the gift by more than three, four, five or six years.

One sort of gift you cannot make and go away happily thinking that, if you survive seven years, all will be well is a gift whereby you continue to benefit in any way from the property you have given away. So you cannot give your house to your children and continue to live in it and not expect to pay any tax. You will have the option of having it still included in your estate for inheritance tax when you die, or paying an additional income tax on its value for the rest of your lifetime.

It is obviously important to make the most use of your nil-rate band. If a husband leaves everything to his wife, then, because the gift is exempt, the nil-rate band is wasted because there is no need for it to be used. Worse, if she dies the next day, her estate has been swollen by what he left her and there is only her nil-rate band to enjoy. If they had both used their nil-rate bands to the full, £114,000 – that is 40 per cent of £285,000 – might have been saved for the family.

Very often, the matrimonial home is the main or a major asset in the estate. If, on the death of a partner or spouse, an amount equal to the nil-rate band is left to a discretionary trust, of which the spouse and children are the beneficiaries, and the trustees of that trust are empowered by the will to accept a spouse's IOU for that amount, the spouse may well be enabled to continue to live in the house. When the spouse dies, the IOU is a debt against his or her estate. In this way the tax on an amount equal to that of the nil-rate band will be saved. Professional advice must always be taken before anyone embarks on a scheme such as this, and, before it can be entertained, they must hold the property as tenants in common and not joint tenants.

You will have seen that there is plenty to occupy the mind once you have retired. The subject is complicated and is frequently subject to change. It is always sensible to seek professional advice before making any irrevocable decisions. Without professional help mistakes may occur that can cause considerable anxiety and prove to be very expensive.

Appendix B

In the Money:
Financial Planning

BY ROGER PARKES, IFA, CHAIRMAN,

RETIREMENT TRUST

It has been said that there are only two financial worries when you retire: either you live so long that you run out of money or you don't live long enough to enjoy it. The ideal, according to some, is to spend your last penny before you take your last breath. This, of course, is an oversimplification of the problem, but it does bring the issue firmly into focus. Retirement is hopefully that time when many of the daily stresses of a working life are removed, when time and effort can best be guided towards having an enjoyable and fulfilling life after work. Getting your finances in order is essential if those long-dreamed-of retirement days are to be realised.

Without the restrictions of work, you will enjoy at least an extra 1,600 hours of free time per year. In reality, you will probably find it is far more that this, when travelling time and time spent thinking about work are taken into account. We need to recognise that we are, on average, living longer and in many cases retiring earlier than ever before, giving a period in retirement of twenty years or more. It is not unusual for the third age to exceed a third of one's life. The government statistics in 2003 showed that in the UK the average life expectancy for a sixty-year-old male was 20.2 years and for a female 23.4 years. It is essential to plan for this and to recognise some of the dangers of failing to so do.

People retiring will have lived through some periods of high inflation and will remember the devastating effect on savings that simply did not keep pace with rising prices. Inflation was high during the 1970s: it ran at over 24 per cent in 1975 and over 15 per cent in 1976. It was not really under control until 1992, when it was down at 2.6 per cent and just 1.9 per cent in 1993. It has remained around these levels ever since, with minor fluctuations.

However, that does not mean inflation is no longer the enemy of the retired. It comes as a surprise to realise that over a period of just twenty years, well within the normal retirement span, £20,000 would, with an inflation rate of

2.5 per cent, have an equivalent value in today's money of only £15,067. It is my belief that in times of relatively low inflation retired people are more, not less, vulnerable, as the effect is insidious and therefore more difficult to recognise; but it is, nevertheless like a disease, eating away at one's capital. Recent rises in the price of energy and council tax have meant that for many in retirement the rate of inflation is well above the published headline rate. This makes careful financial planning all the more important.

Before planning can take place in any meaningful way, it is necessary to do some work on your current financial situation. This means establishing your post-retirement financial status. It is useful to determine what your pension income is likely to be prior to retirement. A forecast of your state benefits can be obtained from the Department of Work and Pensions. You may be able to boost your income by 'making up' contributions to give you the full state pension if you are below the number of years it requires. You should also get a projected figure of any additional expectations, either from your employer or, if you are in a private pension, from your pension provider. The figures may not be the final ones, but they will provide you with the information on which to base your plans.

Post-retirement, your spending pattern may change in many ways. For example, you will not have the cost of travelling to and from work but you may have increased heating bills, as you may be spending more time at home. You may reduce your expenditure on work clothes and cleaning bills but increase it on social activities, as you will now have more time for them. Each person or couple will have different changes due to personal circumstances.

I strongly recommend that you create a projected post-retirement budget. Try to imagine how your life will alter and look carefully at potential changes to your income and expenditure patterns. You will certainly not arrive at a precise figure first time, and your budget will be modified as you settle into your new way of life, but without this information you may be putting your financial security at risk.

Having established your estimated post-retirement situation you can start thinking about how best to use your savings and possibly any lump sum from your pension. To do this you must have some clear ideas about your needs, your aims and your objectives, and, most importantly, your attitude to investment risk.

Your budget figures will tell you whether or not you will require your savings to provide an additional income. If you do need to provide an income, then it is important that you do not seek an income that will erode the value of your capital. It is the maintenance of the real purchasing power of your capital that will be your protection against the evil of inflation in later years. The last thing you want is to be short of money when, at a later time, your needs may increase.

It's not always possible for everyone to make provisions for long-term nursing care, and we all know that the rules keep changing. This is a matter that requires careful discussion within the family and with your financial adviser. It is certainly not for everyone and you must resist some of the overzealous marketing coming from some providers. For others, however, especially those without close living relatives, it may be an essential part of financial planning in retirement.

In putting together your basic financial plan you must take a number of key factors into consideration. First, you must define a *rainy-day fund* to protect you from those unexpected bills such as boiler failure, car repairs or a new roof, and any other equipment failure. You should also look at your *planned capital expenditure* over the next three years. This could be car replacement, a daughter's wedding, a special holiday or home improvements. This is very important, as you need to keep this money accessible and in cash and not be put at the mercy of the performance of the stock market at the time you need the money.

If you do require an income from your investments, it is sensible to have a *further reserve fund*, held in cash, equal to the value of two years' investment income. The reason for this is that it gives you the opportunity to suspend your income from investments during a period of adverse stock market conditions. This is another part of the strategy to protect your capital against inflation.

All planning must have regard to personal aspirations and be based on a realistic level of expectation of the investment returns.

CASH HOLDINGS	INVESTMENTS
Rainy-day fund	Investment portfolio (to meet your income objectives)
Planned expenditure	
Income-protection fund (equal to two years' investment)	

You will notice that cash holdings are separated from investments. That is because they are two quite different asset classes. Cash holdings generate regular interest, whereas investments rely on the performance of the underlying shares. The main reason people invest in shares is that in the longer term, say five years or more, there is a good chance that shares will outperform cash. This is the reward for taking the risks associated with the stock markets. After all, in retirement we are looking at investments for the next twenty-five years based on normal life expectancy. There is a powerful weight of evidence to show that shares will outperform gilts and cash over the longer term and will give a real opportunity to beat inflation.

If the portfolio is right and the cash reserves are in place, then the best thing to do, if there are adverse market conditions, is to adopt a *buy-and-hold* policy and give the markets the time needed to recover. Because of the cash cushion you will not be obliged to turn what is a loss on paper into a real loss by cashing in investments during adverse market conditions. Economies do grow most of the time, so stock markets rise most of the time.

Cash holdings are usually held in banks or building societies. They offer many different types of account. The main distinguishing factor is how much will you have in the account and for how long can you commit to depositing it. The rule tends to be that the more you deposit and the longer you are prepared to leave it untouched, the higher the rate payable will be. Don't forget that the returns will be liable for tax and will normally fluctuate as base rates change.

Another place for cash might be *National Savings products*. They are not suitable for everyone, but may fit in with your objectives and attitude to risk.

Finally there are *gilts*. These are government bonds and offer a fixed rate of return, normally over a set period with a date set for their redemption. The value of the gilt will change as interest rates change and they need to be carefully managed to get the best returns. They can be a useful asset class within a portfolio where income is a high priority.

The investment portfolio has to be constructed to take into account a number of factors. The first is to identify the specific objective of the portfolio. This may be primarily to provide an income, with capital growth as a secondary factor. This could of course reduce the opportunity for protection against inflation but can be appropriate under certain circumstances. It could be used to provide an income to supplement a pension while preserving capital value. Where no income is required at the present time, your investment aim may be for capital growth alone, with an income option at a later date. It could be to make your fund grow with the objective of leaving a nest egg to your children or a good cause.

The objective of the portfolio will determine the mix of underlying assets and choice of funds. For most people, direct investments in shares is difficult and the costs associated with managing such a portfolio can be high, especially with smaller investments. They can also leave the investor with the need to employ an accountant to deal with the associated tax returns. The use of collective investment funds provides the investor with professional management and reduced paperwork. The key here is to identify fund managers with a process and style that will meet your particular requirements.

The next crucial factor to be taken into account is *investment risk*. It is vital that investors give this issue their full consideration. It is often said that investors are driven by two emotions, fear and greed. Either in excess can be disastrous! There is a correlation between risk and reward. For example, you may keep a stash of cash under the bed, It will not grow, nor will it accumulate interest, but you will know it is there. You may put your money on an outsider at the 2.30 at Ascot; you may be very lucky and pick a winner – but you may lose the lot. These may be extremes but they do serve to make the point.

One way to evaluate risk is to identify the maximum gain and loss over a defined five-year period. Lower-risk funds will include With Profits, Defensive Managed, UK Fixed Interest, Distribution Funds and Cautious Managed Funds. Average-risk funds could be Balanced Managed and UK Equity Income. And higher-risk funds could be Stock Market Managed, Global Equities and any specialised markets or single-countries funds.

Where investments are made in overseas funds, there may be the additional risk due to the currency difference. Your adviser will look carefully at your risk profile and recommend suitable funds.

To assess your risk profile, an assessment questionnaire may be used. The combination of risk profile and the aims and objectives of your investment will then be used to construct the portfolio. It is worth noting that the portfolio will need continual review in order to take account of changing economic and investment conditions.

We all feel bombarded by investment advertising in our weekend newspapers, and all the advice given by the pundits writing their columns. There does seem to be, as in all walks of life, a passion for fashions. One day it is specific countries, the next it is buy to rent, and so on. I believe that journalists serve to provide the potential investor with some ideas and they raise many issues of interest, but they should be used only to provide background information to allow you to put questions to your professional adviser about investment opportunities. In retirement you should be looking at sustainable medium-to-long-term investments to meet your needs Remember: only the professional adviser has to carry the responsibility for the advice given; the newspaper columnist does not.

Taxation issues

With the ever more complex taxation system being thrust upon us, it is impossible to go deeply into the tax regime, although a number of matters concerning taxation are also to be found in Reginald Glick's chapter (Appendix A) concerning legal matters. The rule with taxation is to take advantage of all the allowances and tax breaks that are on offer but don't allow the tax tail to wag the investment dog. In other words, you should not be making specific investments to mitigate against tax unless the underlying reasons for the investment are sound.

I know of many cases where investors were lured into making an investment because of the tax benefits, only to discover that the investment failures far outweighed those perceived benefits. There are still some tax benefits to be had from ISAs (individual savings accounts), but we do not know how long they will be allowed to continue.

Inheritance tax

It is staggering how different people view inheritance tax. Some will go to enormous lengths to protect their capital and to give the government as little as possible. Others will take the view that they started with nothing and their children will have what is left; they simply do not wish to get involved.

There is one overriding rule in arranging your affairs to deal with inheritance tax: do not put your own financial security at risk. It is possible for complicated schemes to backfire when one or other offspring takes advantage of overgenerous parents and leaves the parents financially destitute. We all love our children but when Love turns to £ove there can be many serious family disputes. It is imperative not to do anything that could put your financial security at risk. This does not mean that in many cases there are not sensible actions to be taken. To find out how you may benefit from these you should seek the advice of a solicitor.

Financial advisers

We now have, in effect, three categories of adviser: *tied*, *multi-tied* and *independent*. A tied adviser will be able to give advice on the products of one provider; a multi-tied adviser will work from a limited list of selected companies;

and an independent adviser will offer products from the whole market.

Advisers are authorised and regulated by the Financial Services Authority (FSA). They are covered by the Financial Services Compensation Scheme (FSCS). You may be entitled to compensation from the scheme if an adviser cannot meet its obligations. This depends on the type of business and the circumstances of the claim. Most types of investment are covered for 100 per cent of the first £30,000 and 90 per cent of the next £20,000 to a maximum of £48,000.

It is wise to do some detailed preparation before a meeting with an investment adviser. Get a clear idea of your post-retirement financial situation in terms of income, anticipated expenditure, available capital, current investments, future income and so on. The fuller the information you can have available, the more the advice can be tailored to your specific situation. You should also have a well-thought-out attitude to investment risk, as this is very important to the adviser in making recommendations.

The adviser will have to declare the firm's status in terms of tied, multi-tied or independent. I would recommend that you seek independent advice. Also, I would suggest that you use the services of a specialist investment adviser rather than a general practitioner. You can check the status of the adviser on the FSA website (see 'Useful Addresses', Appendix C). In judging an adviser, note how much information is sought and how much care is taken to establish your attitude to risk.

Advisers would not normally rush to any conclusions or recommendations during the first visit. It may take another visit to finalise the aims and objectives and to confirm their interpretation of all the information. Always remember that it is *your* money and you must feel comfortable with their recommendations. If not, discuss them again and ask for changes to be made so that it becomes acceptable.

However, I do counsel against sitting on the fence, unless you have so much cash that you cannot see yourself ever running out with your current lifestyle expenditure. If you are not in that happy position, you must make some provisions to deal with rising costs. Do not succumb to the often fatal disease of 'analysis paralysis'.

In this Appendix, I have tried to give you a basis for an understanding of the issues involved in prudent financial planning and a guide towards some solutions. They cannot take the place of good professional advice in this ever-changing world. Remember: above all else, it is *your* life and *your* money – and it is *your* retirement.

Appendix C

Useful Addresses

British Dietetic Association
Advice on healthy eating in older people
5th Floor
Charles House
148–149 Great Charles Street
Queensway
Birmingham B3 3HT
0121 200 8080
http://www.bda.uk.com

European Health Insurance Card

For medical cover in the EU

(You can pick up an EHIC form from a post office)

EHIC Applications

PO Box 1115

Newcastle upon Tyne

NE99 1SW

0845 606 2030

http://www.dh.gov.uk/travellers

ExtraCare Charitable Trust

Devoted to looking after the elderly including retirement homes

Abbey Park

Humber Road

Coventry CV3 4AQ

024 7650 6011

http://www.hcl.uk.com/test/extracare

Financial Services Authority

25 The North Colonnade

Canary Wharf

London E14 5HS

020 7066 1000

http://www.fsa.gov.uk

Help the Aged

Produces a range of booklets on living in the third age

England:

207–221 Pentonville Road

London N1 9UZ

020 7278 1114

email: info@helptheaged.org.uk

Scotland:

11 Granton Square

Edinburgh EH5 1HX

0131 551 6331

email: infoscot@helptheaged.org.uk

Wales/Cymru:

12 Cathedral Rd/12 Heol y Gadeirlan

Cardiff/Caerdydd CF11 9LJ

02920 346 550

email/ebost: infocymru@helptheaged.org.uk

Northern Ireland:

Ascot House

Shaftsbury Square

Belfast BT2 7DB

02890 230 666

email: infoni@helptheaged.org.uk

Inter Varsity Club (London)

Garden Studios

11–15 Betterton Street

Covent Garden

London WC2H 9BP

020 7240 2525

email: admin@londonvic.com

Medical Advisory Service for Travellers Abroad (MASTA)

Advice on preventative health precautions abroad

http://www.masta.org

NHS Direct

Emergency advice on medical problems

7th Floor

207 Old Street

London EC1 9PS

0845 4647

http://www.dhsdirect.com

REACH

A charity for those seeking voluntary work – for retired
business and professional people

89 Albert Embankment

London SE1 7TP

Tel 020 7582 6543

Fax 020 7582 2423

email: mail@reach-online.org.uk

Retired and Senior Volunteer Programme (London)

A freestanding programme within Community Service
Volunteers organisation

237 Pentonville Road

London N1 9NJ

020 7643 1385

email: rsvpinfo@csv.org.uk

http://www.csv-rsvp.org.uk

Retirement Trust

A charity that provides regular one-day seminars for those retiring, plus seminars for companies and institutions.

Tulip House

70 Borough High Street SE1 1XF

020 7864 9908

email: info@theretirementtrust.org.uk

Royal Institution

Excellent lectures, two or three times a week, on science-related topics for the interested layperson; not necessary to be a member

21 Albemarle Street

London W1S 4BS

020 7409 2992

http://www.rigb.org

Saga

A commercial organisation catering for travel and insurance needs of over-fifties; organises cruises, holidays, insurance (including medical)

The Saga Building

Middelburg Square

Folkestone CT20 1AZ

01303 771 111

http://www.saga.co.uk

University of the Third Age

19 East Street

Bromley

KENT

BR1 1QH

020 8466 6139

http://www.u3a-info.co.uk

Glossary

Acupuncture: Part of Chinese traditional healing. It is based on the belief that there exist certain yin and yang streams in the body. The concept is to rebalance these by releasing or enhancing the power by stimulation, usually using needles, of the various access points around the body. Although it has been suggested that its effects are due to the release of endorphins, this has not been confirmed.

Alternative medicine: A misleading term to suggest that there are various strands of accepted medical practice. There are not. It covers a variety of native, herbal, faith-based and frankly phoney medical practices. If a treatment is effective it is not an alternative: it becomes part of regular medicine.

Aphasia: An inability to enunciate appropriate words. There are various congenital and acquired forms of this impairment. As we get older, our brains may develop a difficulty in accessing a word when it is needed. The more we concentrate, the more difficult it becomes to access the right word.

Blethroplasty: The operation to correct drooping eyelids and remove any bags under the eyes. It is a simple operation carried out under local anaesthetic, and not only can it improve visual fields but it can also make a person appear younger.

Botox: A weak solution of botulinus toxin. Botulinus toxin acts to block specific receptors that are essential for the formation and release of the chemical acetylcholine. This chemical is responsible for carrying messages from one cell to another in the brain and from the brain to the muscles and organs of the body. In high doses botulinus toxin causes paralysis, unconsciousness and death. Injected locally in tiny doses it paralyses the muscles in the area for six to twelve weeks.

CAT scan: CAT stands for *computer-assisted tomography*. These scans allow details of the body's organs to be revealed in pictures taken at a series of predetermined slices throughout a particular part of the body. By this means changes occurring deep inside the body, which would not be obvious in a plain X-ray, can be clearly seen.

Cervical smears: A superficial scraping of the cells of the neck of the womb, which are taken and smeared onto a microscope slide. By examining the cells in the smear, it is possible to detect abnormal cells that may indicate a precancerous or a cancerous condition.

Chromosomes: Strands of DNA within the nucleus of each cell (except the red blood cells) that determine the makeup of each individual. The actual function of much of the chromosome's DNA is unknown.

Decalcification/osteoporosis: As we get older the turnover of calcium within the cells of the bone becomes slower. Osteoporosis is the result of an increase in the loss of calcium that often results from this process. If untreated, it can lead to the collapse of vertebrae and the breaking of bones in the hip and leg

Depression: A depressed state of mind is not necessarily abnormal. There are two main causes of depression: *endogenous* (from within) and *exogenous* (from without). Endogenous depression is nearly always genetically determined and is the more serious form of the disease. Exogenous depression is a reaction to events taking place in the environment, to an acute illness or to drugs. Because this form of depression has a cause that is either curable or removable, it has a much better prognosis. Many acute depressive illnesses prove to be a mixture of a predisposition (endogenous) aggravated by an environmental stress (exogenous).

Detoxification: Toxic and unwanted substances are rendered harmless in the body, either by excretion in the urine (if they are water-soluble), or by being rendered water-soluble by treatment in the liver. A specific liver enzyme system (P450) carries out most of this detoxification process. The process speeds up if it has recently handled the same toxin but its activity cannot be enhanced by any of the current so-called detox programmes. Drinking gallons of water, purging oneself or denying oneself food does not influence the rate of detoxification.

Diabetes: Disease caused by the failure of the islet cells in the pancreas to produce sufficient insulin to maintain a normal blood-sugar level. Insulin turns any excess of sugar into glycogen to be stored by the liver until the blood-sugar level falls. There are two distinct types of diabetes. Type 1 diabetes usually becomes evident in childhood, when the patient fails to put on weight, is always thirsty and passes an excess of urine that often smells like pear drops. This type of diabetes requires insulin treatment. It can be associated with the development of defective vision, renal disease and heart attacks. Type 2 diabetes is rare in children (even in fat children). It is a disease of middle and old age. It is frequently associated with obesity, although in many cases it occurs in slim people. It can often be controlled by a diet of restricted sugar and carbohydrate. If diet fails to control the diabetes, pills are available to assist. Only in relatively few cases is insulin required.

ECG: Electrocardiogram. This follows the electrical activity in the heart as it contracts. It provides valuable information about the rate of the heartbeat, its regularity and the source of any abnormalities. It also provides an insight into any malfunction of the heart or a serious lack of adequate blood supply to its muscle. It does not allow a good assessment of the adequacy of the pumping action of the heart. For this purpose an echocardiogram is required.

Endorphins: Chemicals released into the bloodstream that produce a feeling of contentment and reduce the appreciation of pain. They act on the same receptors in the brain as morphine. They are released in tiny amounts by sunshine and laughter.

E-numbers: Designations given by the EU to food additives that have been passed as safe in up to a hundred times the dose used. Many of them are naturally occurring substances, such as citric acid and vitamin C. They are used to preserve the freshness of foods and to increase flavour and colour.

Equity release: A scheme that allows a home owner to realise some of the increase in the value of their house that has taken place over the last twenty years. It is not without a financial downside but it can provide additional income or finance to those who have retired, especially if they have no children and any inflationary pressures are reducing. It should never be entered into without prudent professional advice.

Free radicals: Essentially, highly positively charged ions that are split off during various biological processes within the cell. They are extremely dangerous to the protein of the cell. They are also formed when the cell is subjected to X-ray, irradiation, high temperatures and high ultraviolet-light exposure. The effect of these radicals can be neutralised *in vitro* by antioxidants, which have a negative charge. It is for this reason that it has been suggested that a great variety of foods are good for you and help to prevent cancer and ageing. There is little evidence that any of these substances, taken by mouth, actually end up inside the cell and neutralise free radicals.

Free-range and organic eggs: Organic eggs come from chickens conforming to the organic rules. They have to be fed organic food for the first six weeks of their lives after which they can be fed the same food as battery hens. They have to be allowed a roaming space of one square metre for every 25lb of chicken. They are not necessarily free range. Free-range birds can eat whatever food they can find and can mix freely. Because of the ability of free range chickens to mix with other livestock and humans it is these birds that are at risk of contracting bird flu and are more likely to be involved in passing it on to humans.

Herbal medicines: There is multibillion-pound business in herbal medicines in the UK. It is improbable that it does much harm but it is even more unlikely that in most cases it does anyone (other than those selling them) any good. Many of the compounds have some pharmacological activity, as do most natural substances, but the potency of these compounds is uncontrolled and variable. There has long been intensive investigation into all claims of medicinal properties in these herbal medicines and wherever an advantage has been demonstrated it has been used to provide a controlled medicine.

Homeopathy: This system of treatment was developed as an alternative to Galenic medicine by a German doctor, Samuel Hahnemann, at the end of the eighteenth century. It was introduced into England by Prince Albert. As presently used, it prescribes smaller and smaller doses of specific medicines that are supposed to antagonise the ill effects of the disease. There is no scientific evidence to support any claim that it is effective. Indeed, in the low doses of active substances used it is doubtful that it has any advantage over water.

HRT (hormone replacement therapy): This was originally introduced to treat the distressing symptoms of the menopause. It was soon realised that it had the potential to prevent the high rate of postmenopausal fractures of the hip. Initially, it sought to replicate the hormonal pattern of menstruating women by using oestrogen followed by progesterone to promote menstrual flow. In so doing, it also prolonged the period of breast activity and the period of vulnerability to cancerous changes. Today, the dose of oestrogen is greatly reduced in most HRT preparations and progesterone is frequently omitted. Studies have suggested that the older preparations used for HRT were associated with a 2 per cent increase in the risk of breast cancer and a significant increase in blood pressure, but this may be offset by a slightly reduced risk of a heart attack. With the availability of alternative methods of preventing osteoporosis, HRT is now being increasingly used to defer the effect of ageing in postmenopausal women. (*See also* oestrogen/progesterone.)

Immune response: The body reacts to foreign protein and pathogenic bacteria and viruses by producing an inflammatory immune response. This involves the production of antibodies by the spleen and the lymphocytes. It is the reaction between these antibodies and the foreign protein that initiates the inflammatory response from the local tissues. As one gets older, these responses become depressed. As a result, bacteria that were quickly dealt with by a young person may establish themselves. This causes an increase in the frequency of infections and reduced inflammation, and, since many of these organisms are less virulent, they are frequently less effectively treated with antibiotics.

Oestrogen/progesterone: These are the two hormones produced by the ovaries of women of childbearing age. They are steroids and they are responsible for producing the feminisation of the body. They have an effect in delaying or slowing some of the ageing processes, especially decalcification of bone. Since their widespread use, hip fractures in women have been greatly reduced. (*See also* HRT.)

Omega-3 fatty acids: Lipids found in highest concentration in oily fish such as salmon, shellfish and mackerel. The concept that they were especially important in maintaining health comes from the finding that they are present in high concentrations in the membranes and walls of the cells in the brain. There has been no confirmation that, in the short term, they provide any advantage to brain power or health.

They may be of especial importance in babies and very young children.

Organic food: Food grown without the benefit of chemical fertilisers and pest control has been shown to be no better, either in taste or nutritional value, than food grown by conventional farming methods. It is about 40 per cent more expensive. The sale of organic food has been promoted by scare stories of the possible harmful effects of the chemicals used in conventional farming. There is no evidence whatever to support this allegation.

Pilates: This is a method of exercise based on maintaining and improving muscle mobility and strength by stretching and bending exercises. It has an established training programme. A surprising number of the exercises are similar to those of routine physiotherapy.

Placebo effect: There is little doubt that belief in the benefit of a particular treatment can alleviate the symptoms of a disease without affecting the underlying disease process. It is far less evident in diseases that have a well-defined pathology and are amenable to recognised medical treatments.

Reflexology: A system of treatment based on the belief that pressure on various parts of the foot produces relaxation and relief of stress. It has no scientific basis.

Retirement Trust: This charity was established almost twenty years ago to encourage preparation for retirement. It organises subsidised one-day symposia and special events linked to the needs of those about to retire. (Tel. 020 7864 9908, email info@theretirementtrust.org.)

Third age: The concept of the third age is relatively new. In years gone by the duration of retirement was so short it hardly qualified for the term *age*. Today, the expectation of twenty to twenty-five years of active life after retirement justifies regarding it as a period of 'new life' to distinguish it from childhood and adulthood.

University of the Third Age (U3A): This started in France as a means of providing an opportunity for taking a postgraduate degree after retirement from active employment. In the UK it is a network of institutes offering both social and intellectual programmes for those over fifty-five years of age.

Valium: This benzodiazepine is widely prescribed as a means of relaxing uptight, overanxious individuals and promoting relaxation. It should be used with extreme caution in the over-sixties, because it readily accumulates in the body, causing drowsiness and disorientation.